How Australian Are You?
A multiple Choice Quiz

By: O. James Younessi

"How Australian Are You?," by Dr. OJ Younessi. ISBN 978-1-60264-268-3 (soft) ISBN 978-1-60264-269-0 (hard).

Published 2008 by Virtualbookworm.com Publishing Inc., P.O. Box 9949, College Station, TX 77842, US. ©2008, Dr. OJ Younessi. All rights reserved. No part of this publication may be reproduced, stored in a retrieval system, or transmitted in any form or by any means, electronic, mechanical, recording or otherwise, without the prior written permission of Dr. OJ Younessi.

Manufactured in the United States of America.

Acknowledgements

SINCERE GRATITUDE IS DUE first and foremost to my brother and mentor, the man to whom I have always looked up, Professor Houman Younessi. It was he who suggested the idea and helped write a few of the questions. He also checked over many of the replies I had fashioned and constructively opined. Houman and I have had so many laughs on the telephone and reminisced every moment of our adolescence and early adulthood in this country, our new home. It has been grouse!

My very gifted nephew despite his heavy school responsibilities has read many of the questions and laughed along with me. It is to him and all young Aussies that I dedicate this work. Be proud of who you are and keep our identity alive no matter how much pressure is brought to bear by Hollywood. I want to hear the terms I compiled with currency of expression. If anybody calls me "dude" I will chuck a flamin' wobbly!

I would like to gratefully acknowledge a real good bloke, Dr. Aalam Samsavar, who took and re-took the test and proof-read the material. He is a Yank and would not know an Australianism if it bit him on the arse. I have taught him many slangs though and he loves them. He has been a superb friend and I thank him for that too. He has further indebted me by drawing the fabulous cover art for the current book.

My mate and long suffering Anaesthetist, Dr. Paul Stewart, has not only been a top bloke for putting up with me and edging me along but for having been subjected to repeated tests and re-tests of the preliminary versions of the *"How Australian Are You?"* manuscript. He has thoroughly enjoyed the effort almost as much as I have! It was also he who suggested a glossary that was promptly appended. By *prompt* I mean four months of nightly work, every night! He also wanted answers/explanations to each question (another three months). I reckon I ought to curse him not thank him!

I thank also Drs. Katelaris and Read both for accepting to be guinea pigs; one wog and the other skip!

Finally and most importantly, I thank all my patients particularly the old codgers whom I engaged in conversation and over the past 15 years squeezed for the last ounce of colloquialism they knew and in the process perplexing my long-suffering secretary. Good on them for being so patient with me.

O. James Younessi
Sydney August 2004

About the Author:

JIMBO IS A WOG; of that there is no argument and he has no objections to being so identified, either. He will begrudgingly accept the descriptor "camel-driver" too but there were no camels in Tehran and yes you could find Tee-shirts, denim Jeans, chocolate, automobiles, etc. However there was no boat involved in his migration to this country and such a suggestion does make him have a spaz attack.

Jim's mother nation, Iran, saw a revolution and a war and much upheaval prompting his parents to migrate to the United States initially and ultimately to Australia. He was a lad of eleven when the exodus out of Iran began. Not knowing any English he attempted the last years of high school in USA and Australia - school books in one hand and dictionary in another - and then trained to become a surgeon.

The references in this book are heavily skewed towards Melbourne and Sydney as these cities are where he spent the bulk of his university education before setting out to England and Ireland to further his surgical training.

He is now in specialist surgical practice in Sydney.

Introduction:

LANGUAGE OF THE STREET (or the school-yard!) is of necessity tainted with many adjectives and adverbs not many of which are flattering. Vulgarities aside one can not "purify" the street tongue and still maintain any sense of what is being conveyed. Even the vulgarities are, used properly, invaluable in crisp delivery of an idea!

Such a "purification" of a language is an abomination of the same caliber as ethnic "purges" we have witnessed in the last century for a language is only beautiful in that it is essentially an experiment unfolding before us.

Imagine there had never been any immigration, no Ned Kelly, no Furphy brothers, the Eureka stockade never occurred, and there was no gold rush, Malcolm Fraser never lost his pants, and no ANZAC digger ever downed a middy or two of beer or played a game of two-up; what would our language be like now? Well it wont be "Strine[1]".

There is much in the spoken language that is neither transmissible nor comprehendible without having been properly subjected to it. I recall arriving in Australia after having, in my own opinion, had an adequate command of English. That day I was supposed to go with the removalists in their truck to our rented house directing

---

[1] "Strine" is a contraction (in accent) of "Australian" to mean Australian English.

4

these blokes to the address. Well, I could not understand a thing they were saying. They were yabbering along in what appeared to be an entirely different language, I might as well have been in Norway! I do distinctly recall thinking I will not be vanquished and one day I will understand *all* that is being said. Sometime later, one of these blokes turned out to be a garbo[2] in our suburb and I did get to speak to him again and this time I could understand him! It dawned on me how subtle and how beautiful a language really is.

In this book I have attempted to capture that beauty and subtlety. Someone said that this day and age one can not joke about anyone other than the young, straight, male, white, protestants! I have never for a moment consciously set out to embarrass or bring about any slight on any race, occupation, sexual orientation, either of the genders, or religious or ethnic groups.

---

[2] A "garbo" is the diminutive form of "garbage collector" or more politically correct- a city council employee.

Abstract:

I HAVE PREPARED A humorous manuscript on the subject of Australian slangs, cultural diversity, and societal make-up. It is an attempt to capture what makes us unique as a nation. The work is well-researched, properly referenced, engaging and humorous. It is also somewhat autobiographical chronicling my journey to become an Aussie.

I am cognisant of the fact that similar books have been published before. Some take the form of a dictionary of terms and others may concentrate on one aspect or another of what makes this nation so wonderful. There are serious works available as are humorous pieces, however as far as I can establish this work is unique in that it presents the material as follows:

1. Four sets of 50 multiple choice questions (200 in total), testing knowledge of a slang word, Australianism, or basic knowledge of the country. The material is new and amusing. The replies are cleverly chosen to frustrate guess-work.
2. A scoring sheet
3. A section where the questions are individually dissected, the correct answer given, and the Australianism upon which it was based explained.
4. A glossary that is specific to this work and thus not overly laborious

There has been lately much made of the Australian Citizenship "test" for the prospective new citizens. I smiled quietly every time I heard such propositions cringing at how many of us could rightly claim to be able to pass these test papers that follow.

The book is intended to entertain and amuse but I am hopeful also teach.

Test Paper One

1. If you are a crow-eater, you are:
    a. A person of limited means obligated to subsist on inferior food stuffs
    b. A resident of South Australia
    c. One who likes eating magpies
    d. Endowed with a loud booming voice

2. Shazza wears track suite pants, thongs on her feet, and a singlet without a bra. She has long thin blonde hair that is wet and roughly combed. She is most likely:
    a. About to be deported as an illegal migrant
    b. Disinclined to "pinch a fag off you"
    c. Applying for a single mother pension
    d. From Toorak or Killara.

3. If you barrack for the Bombers, then you are:
    a. A member of the Royal Australian Air Force
    b. A dilly bag
    c. A fossicker
    d. A supporter of Essendon

4. If you are a flamin' drongo, you are:
    a. A purveyor of furphies
    b. A bloody Galah
    c. An identity
    d. A jumbuck

5. If you go from Melbourne to Sydney, your bathers would become:
    a. Cozzies
    b. Swimmers
    c. Divvies
    d. Flogs

6. What did the Swagman meet by the Coolabah tree?
    a. A Sheila named Matilda
    b. A jumbuck
    c. A young lady by the name of Sheila
    d. A mozzie

7. A bloke wears tight jeans, moccasins on his feet, and a singlet. He has long sparse dirty blonde hair. He is sporting a beanie. Then he is:
    a. Likely to respond to the name Percival
    b. Most probably a Westie
    c. A Barney
    d. Unlikely to be a dole bludger.

8. If you are cutting your neighbour's grass:
   a. You are most likely employed to do so
   b. Are a kind person who is performing an act of charity
   c. You are involved in a secret liaison with his wife
   d. You are a "Top Bloke"

9. Your mate says to you: "It is your Shout...":
   a. He is inviting you to sing
   b. He is inviting you to scream in an exercise to lessen the burden of child-birth
   c. You best buy the next round of drinks
   d. He is letting you have your say.

10. If you go from Melbourne to Sydney, a "Bogan" becomes:
    a. Rather pleasing to the eye
    b. Uninteresting
    c. A Westie
    d. A more frequent sighting

11. You are driving from Melbourne to Sydney using the Hume Highway. You stop at Wangaratta for a couple of sangas. When you start off again you find yourself driving towards Benalla. What must you do?
    a. Get a Chiko Roll quick smart
    b. Drive the porcelain bus
    c. Chuck a Uee
    d. Jump a Joey

12. How many Victorian pots in a New South Welsh middy?
    a. 1
    b. Half
    c. 2
    d. 2.5

13. If you own an FJ, what do you own:
    a. A refrigerator
    b. A Flap Jack
    c. A fat Joey
    d. A Car

14. As famed by Mike Willessee, Who is Shane Paxton?
    a. A purveyor of furphies
    b. A bloody Galah
    c. A jumbuck
    d. *The* Aussie Bludger

15. Davo bought a slab of grog. He gave Johnno 4 tinnies off the slab. How many tinnies left?
    a. None
    b. 20
    c. 16
    d. 2

16. Which expression does *not* mean to "chunder"?
    a. Kerbside quiche
    b. Liquid laugh
    c. Pavement pizza
    d. Dunny tinner

17. Gazza has just chucked a wobbly. Then:
    a. Your mate Gazza is rather daft
    b. Gazza is likely to have been pleased with your performance
    c. Gary has had a spaz attack
    d. She is unlikely to be a dole bludger.

18. Which of these famous Australians was caught with his pants down?
    a. Alan Bond
    b. Christopher Skase
    c. John Howard
    d. Malcolm Frazer

19. If you are a larrikin, you:
    a. Make people laugh
    b. Shear Sheep
    c. Are in the business of making money
    d. Are a killjoy.

20. Which of the following can keep your grog cold?
    a. A Galah
    b. An Esky
    c. A Westie
    d. A Bunyip

21. If your mate Mario was born in Naples, but moved to Melbourne in the 1950s, then he may well be aptly referred to as:
    a. An italic
    b. A Banana Bender
    c. One who likes eating magpies
    d. A Wog

22. Your mates have set you up for a shag. You rock up to find her daggier than a box of blowies. Your next course of action may well be to:
    a.   Roger the nearest warfie
    b.   Say : " Righto, lets have a shonky"
    c.   Head off to the pub quicker than a dilly-bag of prawns in the midday sun
    d.   Either (a) or (b) but not (c).

23. If you are a gum sucker, you:
    a.   Are suffering poor dental health
    b.   Chew tobacco
    c.   Live in Victoria
    d.   You are "sucking face" with Victoria

24. Fill in the missing words: "Aussie kids are……….kids":
    a.   Vegemite
    b.   Tip Top
    c.   Weet Bix
    d.   Cadbury

25. Who hosted the popular game show "*Sale of the Century*" after 1993:
    a.   Glen Ridge
    b.   Tony Barber
    c.   Jana Wendt
    d.   Ray Martin

26. You shout a beer, what are you doing?
    a.   Request a beer loudly to gain the attention of the bar tender
    b.   Your mates must have all gone home
    c.   It is your turn to do so
    d.   Neither of the above

27. A Tramie is unlikely to be:
    a. A Mety
    b. Awake
    c. Drunk
    d. Awake, may well be drunk but is most decidedly a Mety.

28. A Technicolor yawn is:
    a. A wobbly
    b. What you may encounter in the porcelain bus
    c. What you told Ralph on the big white phone
    d. Both (b) and (c)

29. If you are Fair Dinkum, You are:
    a. A Jolly Jumbuck
    b. A dole bludger
    c. Not to be trusted
    d. Unlikely to tell furphies.

30. You are in a bar. A woman asks if she can: "... bludge a smoke off you". What is being said:
    a. Some bloke wants a cigarette
    b. It is the same as some Sheila wanting to steal a ciggy.
    c. The girl reckons you are hot
    d. It is her shout

31. You ring your mate to say, you are "just gonna chuck the lot in"?
    a. You are angry with Charles, and he will have a rude surprise
    b. You are planning to quit
    c. It is your mate's shout
    d. Then life must be good.

32. If you are a Pommie, you are likely to be:
    a. A bloody whinger
    b. A kill joy but not likely to complain ceaselessly
    c. An Italian migrant
    d. A tramie, and you like your beer ice chilled

33. If your mate has had a continuous run of bad luck, then he is likely:
    a. To *not* have killed a Chinaman in a previous life
    b. To shout all his mates to tea
    c. To chuck it all in *or* kill a Chinaman
    d. To chuck it all in *because* he reckons he must have killed a Chinaman

34. Your mom asks you to come and have your tea. She is:
    a. Wanting your dinner not to get cold
    b. Wanting you back as she is about to pour your tea
    c. Asking you to shout
    d. Worried that you have forgotten to "slip, slop, and slap"

35. Jacko asks you to "bugger off". He:
    a. Is inviting you to reconsider your original offer
    b. Is telling you furphies
    c. Cannot be a poofter
    d. Is on the wagon

36. If you are calling Ralph on the big white phone, then:
    a. Ralph must live overseas
    b. You are driving the porcelain bus
    c. You are disinclined to use your mobile phone
    d. All of the above

37. Your mates say, "come on, don't be a bloody poof, have one for the road". Then:
    a. You are being encouraged to date an ugly woman
    b. They have got wind that your old lady has summoned you home
    c. A delicious home cooked meal is out of the picture
    d. You are offered grog prior to departure

38. Which is *not* likely to be crook?
    a. A Queensland politician
    b. A Victorian cop
    c. A used car sales man from Parramatta
    d. The person who has been chased away from the hospital

39. If you are fair dinkum about a deal, you are likely to be:
    a. Tentative
    b. In need of tax relief
    c. Unaware that the bloke is telling you furphies
    d. A killjoy.

40. What is an attribute *not* associated with a jumbuck?
    a. A fleece
    b. Being jolly
    c. A billabong
    d. A Bunyip

41. BHP stands for:
    a. Bloody Horny Poofter
    b. Broken Hill Proprietary
    c. Bigger, Happier, Prettier
    d. Bendigo Harness Puller

42. If you are looking at a "dog's eye and dead horse", you are looking at:
    a. A potential meal
    b. An accident involving farm animals
    c. A woman with a disproportionately large buttocks
    d. A doorknob with a keyhole in the centre

43. A "Uni bloke" is most likely:
    a. A gentleman living in the suburb of Unionville
    b. A student
    c. An employee of the Unilever company
    d. A workers' union representative

44. It is half time at the MCG and you are purchasing a meat pie, which would the canteen attendant not offer you additionally?
    a. Sangas
    b. Snags
    c. Dunny door
    d. Dead horse

45. If your mate's old lady is a good sort, then:
    a. His mother is a kindly and pleasant lady
    b. His wife is pretty
    c. Both (a) and (b)
    d. Neither (a) nor (b)

46. If you have stolen a fag off your old man, then you
    are:
    a. Both poofters
    b. A poofter and he is not
    c. A bludger with an antisocial habit
    d. He is a poofter and you are not

47. Of these, which is a common and very popular
    Australian snack?
    a. Scallops
    b. Dog and Bone
    c. A bush pig
    d. Jones's potato crisps

48. Which of your attributes is likely to be compared
    to a dunny door?
    a. Your broad shoulders
    b. Your loud booming voice
    c. Your rude bits
    d. Your disproportionately large head

49. In Sydney, where will you *least* likely be able to
    find a wog?
    a. Cabramatta
    b. Parramatta
    c. Lakemba
    d. Watson's Bay

50. If you have Buckley's chance of concluding a deal, you had better:
    a. Bugger off
    b. Crack onto the nearest Sheila
    c. Ask terms in writing
    d. Get heaps of grog to celebrate.

Scoring your results:

<u>Count the right answers:</u>

96 – 100%   On ya mate

80 - 95 %   You must be a bloody wog

65 -79%   We see through the fake accent. You are a Kiwi. Dare you to say Six!

51 - 64%   You slept through the bloomin' docos on Australia

< 50%   No there are no bloody Kangaroos in the streets you poof

Test Paper Two

Circle the right 'un answer. Stuff them poofie bastards who wanna have a crack anyway. You got Buckley's of guessing. We wanna avoid you chuckin' ya bloody pencil and havin' a spaz attack. Do not answer from ya bloody arsehole. If you get them all right well then on ya'. Don't be a flamin' Sheila and aveh go.

51. In Melbourne if you "follow the footie", you most likely:
    a. Barrack for the Kings
    b. You are the goal keeper
    c. Barrack for Carlton
    d. You are a sanga

52. Which of the following is not an exclamation:
    a. Streuth!
    b. Bugger!
    c. Flaming hell!
    d. Dunny!

53. If I ask you to take a "Capt'n Cook at my trouble and strife" you are *least* likely to say:
    a. Bugger!
    b. Chuck a left mate
    c. Crikey, you have done well!
    d. She is apples mate

54. Which of these would *not* ordinarily be considered edible?
    a. A Chiko Roll
    b. Sangas
    c. Dogs eyes
    d. A cake hole

55. Jonsey is built like a brick shithouse, then Jonsey?
    a. Is an athletic sort
    b. Has a broad booming voice
    c. Likes his grog
    d. Has a poor constitution and likely to suffer regular fits of wheezing

56. Jacko has just told Davo, that Gazza has the hots for some Sheila. Davo is most likely to reply thus:
    a. Bugger off!
    b. Fair Dinkum?
    c. She is apples mate!
    d. All of the above

57. Modesty aside, where would you *not* relieve yourself?
    a. In a dunny
    b. In a lavvy
    c. On a bunyip
    d. On the footpath in a back alley

58. A snag is?
    a. A sandwich
    b. A rather thick sausage
    c. Not edible
    d. A man likely to frequent pubs

59. A servo is?
    a. A slang word for Army service
    b. Where you buy petrol
    c. The same as a chunder
    d. A bull that has been put to stud

60. If your best mate says of your sister that "she is apples!", which of the following best applies:
    a. It would have to be your shout then
    b. You are duty-bound to invite him to a jumbuck to preserve your family honor
    c. He must have been waltzing with Matilda
    d. You tell him he should have his eyes examined

61. Which of the following is a Western Australian?
    a. A sand groper
    b. A banana bender
    c. A Westie
    d. Lord Fleming

62. I am trying to see to a clandestine liaison with my best friend's sister. A mutual friend sees us. What am I least likely to say:
    a. Bugger!
    b. Struth!
    c. Two shakes of a lamb's tail!
    d. Fair crack, mate!

63. I am flat out like a lizard drinking, then chances are I am a...
    a. Busty woman
    b. Man endowed with a beer gut
    c. Busy person
    d. Dole cheat

64. What is a tucker box?
    a. A slab of grog
    b. Where you may stash your sangas
    c. Not likely to be where your old lady puts your tea
    d. A Wog chariot

65. Which of these is what you would look forward to after a hard day's work?
    a. A coldie
    b. A uee
    c. Pavement pizza
    d. A bogan

66. Where did the swagman alight :
    a. On the jumbuck
    b. In the billy tea
    c. Near the billabong
    d. In Cabramatta

67. Fill in the missing words: "I love...":
    a. Aeroplane jelly
    b. The Bonyip
    c. Weet Bix
    d. Cadbury

68. Who was the unlikely contender for the President of the proposed Australian Republic:
    a. Jana Wendt
    b. Tony Barber
    c. The late Sir Joh
    d. Eddie McGuire

69. Which is *not* a wog chariot in all likelihood?
    a. BMW
    b. Black Monaro
    c. Falcon XB circa mid-late 1970s
    d. A car with fluffy dice

70. If you are likened to a tramie, you are:
    a. Flat out
    b. Flat on your back
    c. Flat broke
    d. Being made fun of for being a bludger.

71. Which do you *not* chuck:
    a. A wobbly
    b. A Uee
    c. A left
    d. A bandicoot

72. If you have had a Barney with your mate, then you are most likely to;
    a. Need a Maxillofacial Surgeon
    b. Be wet
    c. Have had a roll in the hay
    d. Have shared a meal

73. What color was the Australian ONE dollar bill
    a. Purple and white
    b. Green and white
    c. Green and yellow
    d. Brown and white

74. The game involving the location of the security strip within the one dollar bill is called:
    a. Dollar dazzler
    b. Racing the Roos
    c. Blinky Bill
    d. Strip down

75. Who was the chef featured in Healthy, Wealthy and Wise
    a. Belinda Roberts
    b. Ian Hewtson
    c. Rene Rivkin
    d. Jane Roberts

76. The "Skipping Girl" was the trademark of what product?
    a. Gelatin Desert
    b. Ice cream
    c. Vinegar
    d. Olive oil

77. Which of the following is a brand of matches?
    a. Strikers
    b. Red heads
    c. Sparkers
    d. Red Devils

78. Which one is/was *not* a member of the ALP?
    a. Jeff Kennett
    b. John Cain
    c. Kim Beasley
    d. Paul Keating

79. Which is NOT an Australian Bird?
    a. Eastern Rosella
    b. Kookaburra
    c. Bird of Paradise
    d. Lyre Bird

80. If a bloke says that he doesn't like birds, then
    a. He is most likely a pillow biter
    b. He prefers red meat
    c. He is a vegetarian
    d. He can't be a poof

81. Which suburb in Melbourne is the equivalent of Sydney's Penrith?
    a. Caulfield
    b. Kew
    c. Bacchus Marsh
    d. Box Hill

82. If you have just had a biffo, then which of the following is *not* true of you:
    a. You have had a barney
    b. An altercation has transpired
    c. You are a Sheila
    d. There has been a fist fight

83. A ponce is a man who is:
     a. Effeminate
     b. Pretentious
     c. Built like a brick shithouse
     d. Dancing with Matilda

84. If I have gone troppo, then I must be:
     a. On a pleasant vacation in the tropical north Queensland
     b. Apeshit
     c. Flat-out like a lizard drinking
     d. A flaming poof

85. With some personal risk you have managed to get a truckie to look up and say : "Waddya want, mate?" Your reply would be:
     a. Can I scab a lift mate?
     b. Ya reckon I can "pinch a fag off you?"
     c. Bugger off you big poof.
     d. You may reply (a) or (c) but never (b)

86. If I reckon you can't take a trick, then I mean:
     a. You just can not accept a practical joke
     b. You are constantly unlucky
     c. It is your turn to spin in two-up
     d. You can not chuck a flamin' piss-up in a brewery

87. If I call you a shark-baiter, then you must be:
     a. A Fisherman
     b. A raging poof
     c. A surfie
     d. From Townsville

88. If Davo gets his Sheila a prezzie, he can rightly
     expect to receive:
     a. A decent dunny
     b. A bit of pash
     c. A good bunyip on the side
     d. A jumbuck to kill for

89. You are expected to complete a task no matter
     what the personal cost to you. Your task master is
     likely to want you to persist even if it means you
     must undertake:
     a. "Rogering the Duke of York"
     b. "Fighting a Joey"
     c. "Flogging a 100 poofs"
     d. "Taking a sickie"

90. You have just been done over by a grey ghost.
     You have;
     a. Been spooked by an old hag
     b. An old lady has cracked onto you
     c. Failed to chuck a wobbly
     d. The traffic warden has just booked you

91. A yabbo spins you a good yarn in the paddock,
     then it must be that:
     a. A dero has just told you a ferphie
     b. You are through shearing a Merino
     c. You have derived a good income from this
          year's wool harvest
     d. You came second best in a pub-brawl.

92. A pig has just busted your chops, then:
    a. Chances are you are heading to a pub lunch
    b. Your old lady has finally decided to cook you tea
    c. The venue is the MCG and the Melbourne Hogs are the opposition
    d. By all indications you are back on the Ps mate

93. You have been arsed out, that is…":
    a. You have been selected to sing
    b. You have been sacked
    c. You are flat out
    d. You've gone troppo

94. An alkie is most likely to be:
    a. All alone like a country dunny
    b. About to sink a duffer
    c. On the piss
    d. All of the above

95. If I pay dirt on my mates, then I have had:
    a. No end to my bad luck
    b. My swansong
    c. A barney
    d. A biffo

96. A perve is a term describing what?
    a. A lecherous man
    b. A nerd
    c. A dero
    d. A swag

97. You have just chucked a sickie:
    a. It must be Monday
    b. You are a gray-ghost
    c. You are dispassionate about what the day's
        footie match may be
    d. It would be unbecoming to refer to you as
        a bludger

98. A salvo is likely to:
    a. Make your headache go away
    b. Be superior to Bex powder
    c. Ask you for donations
    d. All of the above

99. If I shout you a schooner of grog in Sydney am I
    likely to be more endeared to you than if I bought
    you a pot in Melbourne?
    a. Yes, because I just bought an extra 5 oz of
        beer
    b. No, because I short changed you 5 oz of
        beer
    c. The schooner in NSW is of equal volume
        to a pot in Victoria. I must like you the
        same
    d. Yes, because I bought you an additional 7
        oz of beer

100. I have set up a naughty tonight, chances are:
    a. I get a score between the posts
    b. I am heading to a Pub in Parkville
        (Melbourne University)
    c. A scone and cream is likely
    d. None of the above apply

Scoring your results:

Count the right answers:

96 – 100%   On ya mate!

80 - 95 %   You must be a bloody wog.

65 -79%   We see through the fake accent. You are a Kiwi. Dare you to say Six!

51 - 64%   You slept through the bloomin' docos on Australia.

< 50%   No there are no bloody Kangaroos in the streets you poof.

Test Paper Three

> *Circle the right 'un answer. Stuff them poofie bastards who wanna have a crack anyway. You got Buckley's of guessing. We wanna avoid you chuckin' ya bloody pencil and havin' a spaz attack. Do not answer from ya bloody arsehole. If you get them all right well then on ya'. Don't be a flamin' Sheila and aveh go.*

101. If someone refers to a mate as a cobber, then he is:
    a. A dike
    b. A chum
    c. A bum
    d. A Native of Brisbane

102. A synonym for a *Black stump* is:
    a. Back of Burke
    b. Dog on a tucker box
    c. Back of Beyond
    d. Both (a) and (c)

103. A Box is:
    a. A sheep's pen
    b. Same as a dog's breakfast
    c. Scattered artifacts
    d. All of the above

104. Bikkies means:
    a. Biscuits
    b. Scones
    c. Money
    d. Both (a) and (c)

105. If you go to the "B & S", then you are most likely to:
    a. Be shopping for groceries
    b. Be looking for a shag
    c. Have your car broken down
    d. Be a Kiwi

106. You have been called a *battler*, then:
    a. You must be a dole bludger
    b. You are making piss poor wages
    c. You are rolling in dough
    d. You have bikkies and tea

107. Someone reckons you are a bastard, then:
    a. You must have been born out of wedlock
    b. You are cunning
    c. He must be your mate
    d. All of the above

108. Danno is a banana bender, then he must:
    a. Be from cane toad county
    b. Work in a plantation
    c. Be a flamin' poof
    d. Be a wanker

109. If you take your ankle biter to the aerial ping pong, then
    a. You have taken your dog to the park for a game of fetch
    b. You have taken your tike to the footy
    c. You have taken your wife/girlfriend to a beach volleyball match
    d. You are having sex

110. If you have been called a Septic Tank, then you:
    a. Were not born in the lucky country
    b. Are probably a politician
    c. Are a sand groper
    d. Are endowed with a big belly

111. If you can not "chuck a piss-up in a brewery" you are:
    a. One to sink a duffer
    b. Unable to have a shag in a whorehouse
    c. As good as tits on a bull
    d. All of the above

112. If you are dealing with an Avo this Arvo, then you :
    a. Are probably making guacamole for a party tonight
    b. Are dealing with a person of Eastern European descent
    c. Are dealing with a person of Italian heritage
    d. Are sleeping all day

113. Johno has just bailed Mick up, then:
    a. John has paid for Michael's release from Jail
    b. John has lied for Michael
    c. Michael and John are flaming homos
    d. Michael is getting an ear-bashing

114. A bastard on father's day, will most likely be:
    a. Drinking with the flies
    b. As happy as Larry
    c. Off to the party
    d. The first cab off the rank

115. Sharon just had a bingle, then
    a. She just had sex
    b. She was unfaithful to her husband or boyfriend
    c. She had a homosexual relationship
    d. She had a motor car accident

116. What are bush oysters?
    a. Nasal mucus
    b. Witchetty Grubs
    c. Sheep's testicles
    d. Yabbies

117. Which is the odd term out?
    a. Donger
    b. Doodle
    c. Bitzer
    d. Old fella

118.Mappa Tazzie is a reference to
    a. A map of Tasmania
    b. The box
    c. Both (a) and (b)
    d. Neither (a) nor (b)

119.If your Bush Telly is Cactus, then
    a. Your television is on the fritz
    b. Your campfire is dead
    c. Your Boss is angry at you and it _is_ your fault
    d. You are knocking a journo

120.Davo is giving the Aussie Salute,
    a. He is an ANZAC
    b. The blowies are about to make him spit the dummy
    c. He just relieved himself of some gas
    d. He just made a rude gesture involving his middle finger

121.Your mate has just had a bundy and coke, then he:
    a. Is probably injured
    b. Is probably high
    c. Is on the piss
    d. Is probably arrested

122.If you would not even "shout in a shark attack", then you are
    a. Rather reserved
    b. Not one to make fuss
    c. As tight as a fish's arse
    d. Quietly spoken

123.Mario is holding an item that is Clayton's, then
    a. Mario just got cheated
    b. Mario is a thief
    c. Mario lives in the bush
    d. Mario is probably a doctor or a dentist

124.What does one most probably do with a durry?
    a. Drink it
    b. Smoke it
    c. Beat it
    d. Ignore him/her

125.If you are Figjam, then you are,
    a. All over the place, not well put together
    b. A lesbian
    c. A fruitcake
    d. Up your own arse

126. It's London to a brick that it will be a goer, therefore:
    a. You can go home and forget about it
    b. It may or may not happen
    c. It will certainly happen
    d. It probably won't happen but there is a slim chance

127. Where will the publican serve you a smaller schooner than the one you are entitled to in Sydney?
    a. Brisbane
    b. Adelaide
    c. A schooner is a schooner always the same size
    d. At a servo

128. If something is Shonky, then it is
    a. Dodgy
    b. Teed-up
    c. Bonzer
    d. OK

129. If you are walking to the pub and it is 20 clicks away, then:
    a. You can walk to it in a minute
    b. Chances are you will not be on the piss, any time soon
    c. You have already drunk too much
    d. You have your wife or girlfriend with you

130. Which of these can you completely empty a full stubby into?
    a. A Pot glass in Queensland
    b. A Western Australian Middy glass
    c. A thimble in Adelaide
    d. All of the above

131. To take a squizz is to take a
    a. Leak
    b. Capitan Cook
    c. Whack
    d. Sip

132. If a game is being played at the MCG, then it probably involves,
    a. Stumps
    b. Fairways and greens
    c. The same thing as at the Gabba
    d. Both (a) and (c)

133. A longneck is a
    a. Tallie
    b. Kindie
    c. Bird
    d. Lollie

134. If you are boiling a billy, you are
    a. Getting your goat prepared to service the ewes
    b. Shearing goats
    c. You are urinating in the toilet standing up
    d. You are camping

135. A dingo's breakfast is
    a. Nothing
    b. A big mess
    c. An infant
    d. A bunyip

136. A butcher in Adelaide is like a
    a. Plumber in Melbourne
    b. Middy in Sydney
    c. Brumby in Albury
    d. Boomer in Fremantle

137. Pertaining to Australia specifically, Leyland Brothers were makers of:
    a. Double-decker buses
    b. B grade documentaries
    c. A grade wines
    d. None of the above

138.You are likely to find school of the air at:
    a. A little farm in the middle of nowhere
    b. Kingsford Smith Aerodrome
    c. An open learning centre
    d. RAAF airbase

139.If you would not be dead for quids, then you are:
    a. Fit as a mallee bull
    b. Happy as Larry
    c. In the crapper
    d. Only (a) and (b) are correct

140.You are in Adelaide, then a *floater* is a:
    a. Meatpie in a plate of peas or gravy
    b. Row boat on the Yarra
    c. Plank of wood on the Murray
    d. Both (b) and (c) are correct

141.If you are drinking with the flies:
    a. You are outback
    b. You can not hope any one to shout you
       grog
    c. You are down in the dumps
    d. Some one has dumped on you

142.You have just referred to your sister's new
boyfriend as a "flash Jack", then he:
    a. Is ostentatiously clad
    b. Is by your reckoning a flamin' nancy
    c. Has swaggering behavior
    d. All of the above

143. Which is the odd one out:
    a. Bikkies
    b. Green backs
    c. Quids
    d. The Aussie battler

144. If you are a fiz-gig, you are a:
    a. Police informer
    b. First fleeter
    c. Wog
    d. All of the above

145. If you could "flog a flea across the paddock, go home to tea and then come back and still find him", then:
    a. You are as mad as a cut snake
    b. As stubborn as a mule
    c. You are flat out like a lizard drinking
    d. Your land is parched

146. If you are spoken to thus: " Who is robbing this coach," then:
    a. You are accused of constant interruption
    b. You better have a good explanation
    c. You are polishing the porcelain bus
    d. The slammer awaits you

147. You and your old lady have a kiss and ride system, then:
    a. You are both perves
    b. Your wife keeps the car after she drops you off at the station
    c. She is a good sort
    d. You are a squatter

148.I hand you a kip, then you are:
    a. As mad as a hatter
    b. A chef in the Japanese restaurant
    c. The spinner
    d. Within your rights to king-hit me

149.If something is Jerry-built then it is:
    a. Soundly manufactured
    b. Made in England
    c. A bloody lemon
    d. Not likely to be the Clayton version

150.A Wongi in Sydney is:
    a. A wog elsewhere
    b. A Chinaman in Albany
    c. A yarn
    d. Both (a) and (c)

Scoring your results:

Count the right answers:

96 – 100%   On ya mate

80 - 95 %   You must be a bloody wog

65 -79%   We see through the fake accent. You are a
              Kiwi. Dare you to say Six!

51 - 64%   You slept through the bloomin' docos on
              Australia

< 50%   No there are no bloody Kangaroos in the
              streets you poof

Test Paper Four

Circle the right 'un answer. Stuff them poofie bastards who wanna have a crack anyway. You got Buckley's of guessing. We wanna avoid you chuckin' ya bloody pencil and havin' a spaz attack. Do not answer from ya bloody arsehole. If you get them all right well then on ya'. Don't be a flamin' Sheila and aveh go.

151. If a walloper has done you over, then chances are:
    a. A more handsome man has stolen your wife
    b. You are spending the night in the remand centre
    c. Your money was on the wrong greyhound
    d. All of the above

152. A grunter is a:
    a. Hot rod
    b. Meal of beans and sausages
    c. Cheap harlot
    d. Trendy man taken to showing off

153. What is a "wood and water Joey?"
    a. A baby boomer just after he will leave his mother's pouch permanently
    b. A bloke who does the menial tasks at the station
    c. A person down in his luck
    d. A carpenter

154. If you have been served up grouse tucker, you will be:
    a. Excused for having chucked a spaz attack
    b. Greatly satiated
    c. Needing a decent meal
    d. Doubtless having bikkies and tea

155. A tomahawk is likely to get:
    a. The sack
    b. Promoted
    c. Your hair singed
    d. A yank on your back

156. What is a dumper?
    a. A privy
    b. That which assures a grouse wipe-out
    c. A pommy
    d. A police informer

157. Which of the following is an occupation?
    a. Postie
    b. Milko
    c. Sparkie
    d. All of the above

158. A forlorn hope of success is:
    a. Buckley's chance
    b. London to a brick
    c. A wiped cat's testicles
    d. Digger's rest

159. If you are as full as a goog, then you will be disinclined towards a:
    a. Home-prepared tea
    b. Smoko
    c. Bonza bloke
    d. Cracker of a Joke

160. Your mate is out back for a *big spit*, then :
    a. He is having pavement pizza
    b. The dunny must have been available
    c. He must be a keen bush-walker
    d. He is likely to be made a lot more popular with the birds upon return

161. Johno is spitting chips, he is likely to be:
    a. Mulching the garden
    b. Blowing his stack
    c. Issuing forth a son
    d. Having a chunder in the dunny

162. If all is crook in Muswellbrook, then:
    a. You should not go apeshit
    b. You are as full as a boot
    c. You are well advised to get on your neddie
    d. Bob is your uncle

163. "Nanna's" are:
    a. What Queensland is famous for
    b. A reference to retirement homes
    c. To be harvested in large numbers in Tasmania
    d. Both (a) and (b)

164. You are discussing the "awnings over the toy shop" then you are likely to be:
    a. Contemplating the purchase of the business
    b. Taking the piss out of your mate
    c. A peeping tom
    d. Canvassing for a new job

165. If I go crook at you, then I am
    a. Spitting chips
    b. Chucking a wobbly
    c. Likely to spit the dummy
    d. All of the above

166. A mollydooker is:
    a. A girl with a bad reputation
    b. A left handed person
    c. Out in the never-never
    d. One who has a roaring trade

167. Your balls (gonads) can be aptly referred to as:
    a. Avos
    b. Acres
    c. Arvos
    d. Abos

168. If you are knackered, you are
   a. Buggered
   b. Nana'ed
   c. Fit as a fiddle
   d. Laughing your arse off

169. What is likened to a cut snake?
   a. A month of Sundays
   b. A bloke who is short
   c. A woman who has accused her husband of indiscretion
   d. One who is as funny as a fart in a lift

170. If I threaten to punch you in the moosh, then you:
   a. Had better nick off
   b. Would be a mollydooker
   c. Must be a pearler
   d. Are a good sport

171. If someone bangs like a bloody dunny door, that person has:
   a. A big spit
   b. Questionable moral standing
   c. Sloppy Joe
   d. A Shank's pony

172. If I am a tat shirty, then chances are I am:
   a. Cruising for a good shag
   b. Aching for a biffo or barney
   c. Gonna get a flamin' good root
   d. Both (a) and (c) are correct

173. If you are a couple of tinnies short of a slab, then:
     a. I wont shag you with my mate's donger
     b. You are a few snags shy of a barbie
     c. You are going twenty to the dozen
     d. You are likely to bang like a dunny door

174. What is a dead cert?
     a. A bounced cheque
     b. A boomerang
     c. Sure thing
     d. A mortician

175. If you pull up stumps in a bloody hurry, you are:
     a. Off like a bride's undies
     b. Hitting the frog and toad
     c. Aptly comparable to a Bondi tram
     d. All of the above

176. Your plate of meat is called into action, you are getting:
     a. Pissed as a parrot
     b. By without your car
     c. A rudie
     d. Your laughing gear used with impunity

177. If you are getting a backroom waltz, then:
     a. You are regretting the Indian meal you consumed earlier
     b. You hadn't blown your brass on flowers and lollies
     c. Things are crook in Muswellbrook
     d. A dilly-bag is in order

178. Which does not pertain to a fart?
    a. To cut the dog in half
    b. To be as dry as a dead dingo's donger
    c. To Drop your guts
    d. Dutch oven

179. A mystery bag, is:
    a. A sausage
    b. A prezzie
    c. Your surprise Easter show bag
    d. A blind date

180. Your missus has just gone crook at you:
    a. Your wife is unwell
    b. She just found lippie on your collar
    c. You will surely get a leg over
    d. None of the above

181. To "come the raw prawn" is to be a:
    a. Smelly person
    b. Quack
    c. Rookie
    d. Road train

182. Rafferty's rules implies:
    a. A dingo's breakie
    b. A dog's breakfast
    c. Tidiness
    d. Rigid discipline

For question 183 – 188, consider the following scenario:

Berko, Stevo, Bruce, Timothy, and Chuck are at the bar having a yarn over a couple of coldies. Bruce has just claimed to have shagged a rather grouse bird.

Jonsey over hears the conversation. Answer the following questions:

183. Pertaining to Bruce what is likely true:
    a. He will be a grumble-bum
    b. He will be like a pork chop in a synagogue
    c. He may be likened to a rat with a gold tooth
    d. It is his shout

184. Which of the men is most likely a Seppo?
    a. Bruce
    b. Chuck
    c. Timothy
    d. Neither

185. How would Jonsey *not* address the quorum?
    a. Bull-fuck!
    b. Fair dinkum?
    c. You beaut....Bruce baby!
    d. You're a rellie, mate!

186. Which would *not* be an apt reply to Jonsey?
    a. Too true
    b. Aah, G'day you big poof
    c. Paper yabber
    d. Watta' ya' reckon?

187. Based entirely on the names, who is likely to be the most aggressive of the men:
    a. Timothy
    b. Bruce
    c. Berko
    d. Jonsey

188. What has Bruce actually achieved?
    a. He has shot an uncommon fowl
    b. He is pissing in his mates pockets
    c. Bruce is all sorted with a good sort
    d. Bruce is likely to be as ugly as a box of blow-flies

189. You are in the dunny choking the brown dog, what would be in order?
    a. A pack of turd tickets
    b. A big spit
    c. Both (a) and (b)
    d. Neither (a) nor (b)

190. If you had to "use the Jerry 'cause the John is Cactus", what has just transpired?
    a. You had to rely on your intuition since the hired hand was unable to perform the requisite task
    b. Since your toilet was broken you were obligated to use a chamber-pot
    c. A hit man was hired to rid you of the problem that the authorities could not effectively address
    d. A threat was not effective and thus frank violence is called for.

191. Joe Bloggs had his Jocks down when a Joe Blake surprised him. What happened?
    a. Some bloke was having a shit when a snake slithered by
    b. Mr. Bloggs was having a root when his lover's husband presented
    c. A baby kangaroo has been surprised by a rattle snake
    d. The first title fighter was caught off guard by the second boxer

192. An ocker is meeting a wog's oldies, he is most likely to say:
    a. G'day you old poof
    b. Sorry I rocked up in my jocks
    c. G'day, Aya gawoing?
    d. Nice knickers!

193. A poddy dodger is playing possum, chances are:
    a. He was seen to have been negligent
    b. He has lost his marbles
    c. He is after favors
    d. A crocodile is involved

194. If you sit on a beer, you are likely to have:
    a. Questionable conduct
    b. Short arms and deep pockets
    c. Lots of mates
    d. Hemorrhoids

195.How are a thingamajig, thingemebob, and thingo different?
    a.   They are all watchamecallits
    b.   Thingo is the same as thingamabob but the opposite of thingamajig
    c.   Both (a) and (b) are correct
    d.   Two thingamajigs makes one thingo

196.If you look pretty swank, you are:
    a.   A bit of a scrubber
    b.   Scrubbing up alright
    c.   Definitely a purse-carrying nancy boy
    d.   You routinely swindle unsuspecting persons

197."Stone the crows what blooming drover's dogs?!" means:
    a.   I am awe inspired by the sheep dog
    b.   I am besotted by the elegance of the item of lingerie
    c.   An anguished displeasure at the inaptitude of the dog
    d.   A cry of joy at the number of attendees at your function

198.You have invited Jacko to a party and tell your mutual mate about it. His reply is: "Pigs bum! He is a piker". Imagine this mate is fair dinkum and in the know, then:
    a.   Jacko will probably get drunk in your party the way he always does
    b.   He will probably not come
    c.   He has a reputation for late arrival
    d.   The mate is joyous at the prospect of seeing Jacko who has a reputation for being the life of the party

199. A lady muck is a:
    a. Woman with airs and graces but no substance
    b. Half empty glass of beer
    c. Glass of beer poured from the bottom half of the beer bottle
    d. Pack of lamingtons

200. Where does Dame Edna live?
    a. Mont Albert
    b. Marriot Lakes
    c. Moonie Ponds
    d. Mosman

Scoring your results:

Count the right answers:

96 – 100%   On ya mate

80 - 95 %   You must be a bloody wog

65 -79%   We see through the fake accent. You are a
Kiwi. Dare you to say Six!

51 - 64%   You slept through the bloomin' docos on
Australia

< 50%   No there are no bloody Kangaroos in the
streets you poof

Answer Key

1. If you are a crow-eater, you are:
    a. A person of limited means obligated to subsist on inferior food stuffs
    b. A resident of South Australia
    c. One who likes eating magpies
    d. Endowed with a loud booming voice

*The correct answer is (**b**).*

The residents of South Australia are referred to as crow-eaters. This epithet is applied based on the fact that the outback South Australia has many crows.

2. Shazza wears track suite pants, thongs on her feet, and a singlet without a bra. She has long thin blonde hair that is wet and roughly combed. She is most likely:
    a. About to be deported as an illegal migrant
    b. Disinclined to "pinch a fag off you"
    c. Applying for a single mother pension
    d. From Toorak or Killara.

*The correct answer is (**c**).*

The description is one of a female "bogan" or a "Westy". Such an individual is not likely to be able to afford to live in the very well-to-do suburbs of major cities which is what option (d) is alluding to. Toorak is a posh Melbourne suburb as is Killara (upper north shore of Sydney).

It would be a common habit for such a person to smoke cigarettes, probably the funny ones too! To "pinch a fag" being to borrow a cigarette.

Bogans are a little like the hippies of the 1960s and often subside on government hand-outs.

"Shazza" is an all too common nickname given to Sharon, which is a popular name with bogans.

3. If you barrack for the Bombers, then you are:
    a. A member of the Royal Australian Air Force
    b. A dilly bag
    c. A fossicker
    d. A supporter of Essendon

The correct answer is (d).

This question pertains to the Australian Rules Football, which was for sometime called Victorian Football League (VFL) but lately is given the acronym AFL as non-Victorian teams have sprung up. The question is impossible to get wrong in Melbourne unless you have been deaf, blind (and stupid).

You will be approached by perfect strangers who may ask: "Follow the footie?" promptly followed by: "Who do you barrack for?"

To follow the footie is to be an avid follower of the game. You barrack or support a particular team, which had better be the same as the person who made the enquiry, if you want to avoid a Barney[3]! Bombers are the moniker for the Essendon team due probably to the fact the old military airport (now multipurpose) airport is located here.

---

[3] Barney or Biffo is an altercation

Choice (a) is an attempt to confuse.

A dilly bag is an Aboriginal word for a small container.

A fossicker is a prospector, one who looks for gem stones, mainly opals.

4. If you are a flamin' drongo, you are:
    a. A purveyor of furphies
    b. A bloody Galah
    c. An identity
    d. A jumbuck

The correct answer is (b).

A drongo is an idiot, intended as an insult more often than a friendly tease. The adjective "flaming", "bloody" or "blooming" is intended simply to exaggerate the characteristic.

A galah is actually a native bird of the parrot family but is intended to mean an ass or a nincompoop. Witness the saying: "As mad as a gum tree[4] full of galahs!".

A furphy is one Australianism you should learn! It means a lie or a deliberate perversion of what you are holding out to be just. Furphy brothers were suppliers of water carted by horse-drawn carriages originating from Shepparton, Victoria. So far so good! Opinion diverges as to how a furphy became a lie. Some say the ANZAC[5] soldiers of WWI would gather around the carts and tell tall stories, a bit like Chinese whispers these would become serious fabrications. Others believe the Furphy brothers never kept their promised appointment for delivery of water.

A jumbuck is simply a sheep! It may have been "jump-up" but I am speculating only.

---

[4] A gumtree is a eucalyptus tree

[5] ANZAC is an acronym for *A*ustralian and *N*ew Zealand *A*rmy Corps

5. If you go from Melbourne to Sydney, your bathers
    would become:
    a. Cozzies
    b. Swimmers
    c. Divvies
    d. Flogs

*The correct answer is (**a**).*

*"Cozzies" is a bastardization of the word
"costumes" as in swimming costumes. Bathers, swimmers
or trunks means the same thing.*

*To "flog" is to sell a dubious item or get rid of
something you know is no bloody good. It could also
mean to steal or "borrow".*

I haven't the foggiest[6] what Divvies are!

6. What did the Swagman meet by the Coolabah
    tree?
    a. A Sheila named Matilda
    b. A jumbuck
    c. A young lady by the name of Sheila
    d. A mozzie

*The correct answer is (**b**).*

*Andrew Barton Paterson was the son of a Scottish
immigrant and was born on February 17, 1864, near
Orange, New South Wales. He became acquainted with
the colorful bush characters that he wrote about so
vividly in his later life from this region of Australia.*

*His pseudonym, "The Banjo", was the name of a
racehorse his father had once owned and reflects his love
for horses about which he has written many poems. His
writing was sympathetic to the landscape and its people.*

---

[6] Implying not having even the foggiest of an impression or insight,
being clueless.

He has created Australia's unofficial national anthem sung in patriotic unison in most sporting arenas called the "Waltzing Matilda[7]". This question revolves around that poem and you may review the poem in the appendix where the references to the poem are italicized.

A swagman is actually a wanderer. A swag is booty or loot and is actually what an English thief may have been after, all those years ago. In this context, a swag is a bag usually of canvas in which you may keep your belongings.

Matilda is a reference to a bed-roll, a sleeping bag. Lately some have also extrapolated this to mean the swag-proper. I'd be buggered if I know where the bloomin' thing came from![8]

A coolabah tree is a shady tree with a high canopy beneath which the swagman rested.

A "mozzie" is simply a mosquito and a "Sheila" is a slang term to describe a woman, any woman. I warn all you men not to use this term near any woman as it has recently become quite abominable. Oddly anyone over 40 could use the term and get away with it but younger men could find themselves needing the services of an Urologist!

If you still do not know what a jumbuck is you have not been paying attention (read back).

---

[7] Given the importance of this poem, it appears as an appendix at the end of this book.

[8] This expression means the same as not having the foggiest!...and I'd be buggerd if I will explain again the adjective. Keep reading for "bugger" though!!

7. A bloke wears tight jeans, moccasins on his feet, and a singlet. He has long sparse dirty blonde hair. He is sporting a beanie. Then he is:
   a. Likely to respond to the name Percival
   b. Most probably a Westie
   c. A Barney
   d. Unlikely to be a dole bludger.

The correct answer is (b).

I have just described the male version of Shazza from question 2.

The term "bloke" is applied without any consequence to an Australian man in stark contrast to the term "Sheila", above. If a man would be a misogynist to have addressed a Sheila thus; does that not make a woman a mysandrist for calling a bloke, bloke?

Moccasins in Victoria are ugg boots elsewhere and are an unflattering article of footwear. A beanie is a hat such as a skier may wear.

A bogan will never be called Percival, which is probably the poofiest[9] name a boy could have. That is not to say that all parents know ahead of time that their son will be a bogan and avoid the name "Percival", but that all Bogan Percivals are naturally selected against per the Darwinian theory.

A bogan in Melbourne, as just described, is a Westie in Sydney. This being a reference to the western suburbs, which is were they are likely to live.

A "barney" is a fight or altercation and a "dole bludger" is a person on social security benefits (government hand-outs). The hand-out being the dole and a bludger strictly defining a lazy person, a loafer.

---

[9] Poofie means, in this context, effeminate. Poofie pertains to poofter, which really means a homosexual man.

8. If you are cutting your neighbor's grass:
    a. You are most likely employed to do so
    b. Are a kind person who is performing an act of charity
    c. You are involved in a secret liaison with his wife
    d. You are a "Top Bloke"

The correct answer is (c).

This term also variably called "to cut someone's lunch" is to move in on someone's wife. I guess it takes its origin from cutting the grass from under someone's feet.

A "top bloke" is a good guy. A man you are proud of or pleased with, a good guy.

9. Your mate says to you: "It is your Shout...":
    a. He is inviting you to sing
    b. He is inviting you to scream in an exercise to lessen the burden of child-birth
    c. You best buy the next round of drinks
    d. He is letting you have your say.

The correct answer is (c).

In this context, the mate is your buddy, your pal, not your wife. This term (noun) as in mateship or comradely behavior is the source of many disastrous events. Like: "common mate, ask that bird out!" or "Don't be a whimp mate, you can drive faster than that" and so on. To "shout" is to "treat" typically to a round of drinks.

10. If you go from Melbourne to Sydney, a "Bogan" becomes:
    a. Rather pleasing to the eye
    b. Uninteresting
    c. A Westie
    d. A more frequent sighting

64

The correct answer is (c).

A bogan as has already been illustrated is the same sort of individual in Sydney or Melbourne save for the fact that in Sydney they tend to reside in the west where, I presume, the real estate is more promising, hence the term "Westie". As far as I can establish there are no more or less per capita bogans in either city making the response (d) incorrect.

11. You are driving from Melbourne to Sydney using the Hume Highway. You stop at Wangaratta for a couple of sangas. When you start off again you find yourself driving towards Benalla. What must you do?
    a. Get a Chiko Roll quick smart
    b. Drive the porcelain bus
    c. Chuck a Uee
    d. Jump a Joey

The correct answer is (c).

This calls first and foremost for some knowledge of Australian geography. The Hume Highway is now, for the most part a carriageway that by-passes most of the little cities between Melbourne and Sydney. In the old days the highway passed through the city of Glenrowan(of Ned Kelly fame[10]).

You have just stopped for sandwiches, since Benalla is closer to Melbourne than Wangaratta, then as you re-commence your journey you must be going the wrong way and a U turn is needed. This is a "uee" and to chuck (or throw) a right, left, or U turn is the colloquial way of referring to these moves.

---

[10] *Ned Kelly was an outlaw bushranger of Irish migrant background who was captured in this town.*

A Chiko roll is a snack. The jumping of Joey achieves you nothing more than the wrath of the boxing kangaroo mother of the aforementioned Joey. This being a term ascribed to a baby kangaroo.

Now to "drive the porcelain bus" is to chuck or chunder; that is to vomit. The image of a person with both hands over the porcelain toilet bowl heaving has been, I reckon, very cleverly compared to driving a porcelain bus.

12. How many Victorian pots in a New South Welsh middy?
    a. 1
    b. Half
    c. 2
    d. 2.5

*The correct answer is (**a**).*

In New South Wales a middy is a 10oz measure of beer. A pot in Victoria carries also 10oz in the old measure.

13. If you own an FJ, what do you own:
    a. A refrigerator
    b. A Flap Jack
    c. A fat Joey
    d. A Car

*The correct answer is (**d**).*

A Joey is a baby kangaroo and reply(c) is clearly intended to confuse the uninitiated. FJ refers to FJ Holden being a local make of car.

14. As famed by Mike Willessee, Who is Shane
    Paxton?
    a. A purveyor of furphies
    b. A bloody Galah
    c. A jumbuck
    d. *The* Aussie Bludger

The correct answer is (d).

A bludger is nowadays applied to anyone who is just lazy. As initially intended it was to refer to one who would live off the wages of another though being fully capable of drawing an income of their own legitimately. Shane Paxton's claim to fame was never having worked a day in his life! He had lived solely on the social security benefits (the dole) his entire life.

15. Davo bought a slab of grog. He gave Johnno 4
    tinnies off the slab. How many tinnies left?
    a. None
    b. 20
    c. 16
    d. 2

The correct answer is (b).

A slab contains 24 cans (or tins) of beer, affectionately called "tinnies".

16. Which expression does *not* mean to "chunder"?
    a. Kerbside quiche
    b. Liquid laugh
    c. Pavement pizza
    d. Dunny tinner

The correct answer is (d).
To chunder is to vomit.

The only odd one is that which pertains to an outhouse, choice (d).

17. Gazza has just chucked a wobbly. Then:
    a. Your mate Gazza is rather daft
    b. Gazza is likely to have been pleased with your performance
    c. Gary has had a spaz attack
    d. She is unlikely to be a dole bludger.

The correct answer is (c).

Gazza is an affectionate way of referring to a person named Gary. It will be inappropriate for his secretary or his boss to call him that, though just about everyone else and the drover's dog can do so safely. This makes choice (d) clearly wrong.

A spaz attack is literally a spastic fit based on the unfortunate belief that all people with spasticity have suboptimal intelligence.

18. Which of these famous Australians was caught with his pants down?
    a. Alan Bond
    b. Christopher Skase
    c. John Howard
    d. Malcolm Frazer

The correct answer is (d).

Malcolm Frazer was a Prime Minster of the 1980s who was locked out of his hotel room with his pants down. I guess he will never live this one down!

19. If you are a larrikin, you:
   a. Make people laugh
   b. Shear Sheep
   c. Are in the business of making money
   d. Are a kill joy.

The correct answer is (a).

A "larrikin" is a happy go lucky sort of a youth.

This Australianism despite being simple, I am having difficulty explaining. You need to see one in action. This person is typically a bit of a diamond in the rough, a little naughty, a bit of a practical joker without being harmful.

Look it up in a thesaurus and you will probably find "anarchist;" but this is not quite right either.

A killjoy is a boresome fellow, a wowser.

20. Which of the following can keep your grog cold?
   a. A Galah
   b. An Esky
   c. A Westie
   d. A Bunyip

The correct answer is (b).

An Esky is a mobile cooler much the same way that the Coleman cooler works. This is known also as the icebox, but most elderly Aussies will think an icebox is a refrigerator. No one will go to a picnic without an Esky full of grog.

A bunyip is a monster of aboriginal legends reputed to haunt brooks and watering holes. Sick of cuddly Koalas, the docile wombat and the other peaceful animals, the white man was very keen to find a vicious Australian animal. They found a skull, which fulfilled the characteristics near a dry creek bed. It even had only one eye socket. They dispatched this off to England and called it the "bunyip". It turned out that it was nothing more than a diseased horse skull! The specimen is now at the Hunterian Museum of the Royal College of Surgeons, London. Do not worry, we do have sharks, crocodiles, snakes and spiders that can do you over before you can say "Crickey, what the…!"

21. If your mate Mario was born in Naples, but moved to Melbourne in the 1950s, then he may well be aptly referred to as:
    a. An italic
    b. A Banana Bender
    c. One who likes eating magpies
    d. A Wog

The correct answer is (d).

*A wog used to be an acronym for **W**esternized **O**riental **G**entleman and really meant a Chinese individual. It now broadly defines any Australian not of an Anglo-Saxon origin. More specifically, it should (and is) used to describe an Eastern European migrant, Middle Eastern, Italian, or any migrant that does not have blonde hair and blue eyes.*

Perversely, it is gaining not only a sort of quasi-approval but to be wog is becoming a trendy commodity[11].

---

[11] See also question 151.

22. Your mates have set you up for a shag. You rock
    up to find her daggier than a box of blowies. Your
    next course of action may well be to:
    a. Roger the nearest warfie
    b. Say : " Righto, lets have a shonky"
    c. Head off to the pub quicker than a dilly-
       bag of prawns in the midday sun
    d. Either (a) or (b) but not (c).

The correct answer is (c).

*A "shag" is sexual intercourse. In this context it is
intended to mean that your friends have set you up to
meet a girl on a blind date. In effect you may potentially
be able to achieve this desired effect but by no means
could it be considered a sure bet.*

*A "dag" is strictly faecal material that sticks to a
sheep's fleece. Daggy pertains to dag and describes
something highly unpolished or looking entirely non-
trendy. It can also be a term of endearment when used by
a friend, like: "You are such a dag Steve, of course you
can borrow my car". The present context however uses
dag in the sense of ugly or poorly dressed which is
likened to a box of blow-flies; that is really ugly.*

*The question is asking what might you do if you front
up to a blind date and discover that the girl is truly
undesirable.*

*To "Roger" someone is to have sex with that person,
however a warfie is the name given to a dockyard worker,
and a bloke would be ill-advised to shag such a person.*

*Something "shonky[12]" is hastily put-together and
generally sub-optimal. The saying means: "Okay, let's
have something poorly made". Clearly this makes no
sense and it was chosen to confound the non-attentive.*

---

[12] See also question 128

The correct thing to do would be to head off to the pub as quickly as possible and the haste with which this is done is likened to how quickly a bag of prawns go off in the midday sun.

23. If you are a gum sucker, you:
    a. Are suffering poor dental health
    b. Chew tobacco
    c. Live in Victoria
    d. You are "sucking face" with Victoria

The correct answer is (c).

Gum sucker is a reference to eucalyptus trees (gum-trees) which incidentally, I reckon, are no more or less abundant in Victoria, than elsewhere in Australia.

Residents of Victoria are known also as "Mexicans". This is because they live south of the Murray River.

In case it is not clear to you "sucking face" or a "tonguie" implies French-kissing!

24. Fill in the missing words: "Aussie kids are..........kids":
    a. Vegemite
    b. Tip Top
    c. Weet Bix
    d. Cadbury

The correct answer is (c).

Weet bix are a popular breakfast cereal and the words complete a commercial jingle.

25. Who hosted the popular game show "*Sale of the Century*" after 1993:
    a. Glen Ridge
    b. Tony Barber
    c. Jana Wendt
    d. Ray Martin

*The correct answer is (**a**).*
  These people are all TV presenters and/or game show hosts. Only Tony Barber and Glen Ridge hosted the programme and Glen replaced Tony.

26. You shout a beer, what are you doing?
    a. Request a beer loudly to gain the attention of the bar tender
    b. Your mates must have all gone home
    c. It is your turn to do so
    d. Neither of the above

*The correct answer is (**c**).*
  To shout anything is to treat someone, or pay for someone else. You would only treat people to beer if they all took a turn, too.

27. A Tramie is unlikely to be:
    a. A Mety
    b. Awake
    c. Drunk
    d. Awake, may well be drunk but is most decidedly a Mety.

*The correct answer is (**d**).*
  Trams are "cable-cars" to Americans.
  Melbourne is the only city that has kept and in some instances enlarged its network of electrified trams. Elsewhere they may run as tourist attractions only.

Melbourne Transportation system includes buses, trams, and trains and is called " the Met". Its employees are "Meties". A tram-driver is a "tramie" and by default also a "Mety". They are said to be particularly lazy.

28. A Technicolor yawn is:
    a. A wobbly
    b. What you may encounter in the porcelain bus
    c. What you told Ralph on the big white phone
    d. Both (b) and (c)

The correct answer is (d).

A Technicolor yawn is to vomit. "To call Ralph on the big white phone" is a reference to the sound of heaving one makes over the toilet bowl, which is also likened to driving a porcelain bus. This I always took to be how one may kneel over the bowl hold the rim with his hands and spew.

29. If you are Fair Dinkum, You are:
    a. A Jolly Jumbuck
    b. A dole bludger
    c. Not to be trusted
    d. Unlikely to tell furphies.

The correct answer is (d).

A "fair dinkum" person is on the straight and narrow. It literally means a trustworthy person or broadly "the truth".

30. You are in a bar. A woman asks if she can: "…
    bludge a smoke off you". What is being said:
    a. Some bloke wants a cigarette
    b. It is the same as some Sheila wanting to
       steal a ciggy.
    c. The girl reckons you are hot
    d. It is her shout

The correct answer is (b).

"Smokes" and "ciggies" are cigarettes. In this context "to steal" or "bludge" means to borrow never intending to replace but this is not malicious. This time the word bludge does not have the connotation of lazy, or loafer that one sees in the context of dole bludging.

Reply (a) does refer to the bumming of a cigarette by a bloke (a man) but the question specifically refers to a woman in the bar. It is therefore wrong.

31. You ring your mate to say, you are "just gonna
    chuck the lot in"?
    a. You are angry with Charles, and he will
       have a rude surprise
    b. You are planning to quit
    c. It is your mate's shout
    d. Then life must be good.

The correct answer is (b).

You are simply saying you plan to throw everything in or walk away vanquished.

32. If you are a Pommie, you are likely to be:
    a. A bloody whinger
    b. A kill joy but not likely to complain ceaselessly
    c. An Italian migrant
    d. A tramie, and you like your beer ice chilled

The correct answer is (a).

*A pom (or pommie) is actually correctly a Pohm, which is an acronym for a **P**risoner **of H**is (**H**er) **M**ajesty and refers to those transported to Australia in the convict ships. Presently it is a mildly derogatory term to refer to the English, who still constitute the largest migrant population to Australia.*

The English are reputed to be an unhappy bunch and would readily "whinge," that is to complain. They are not uncommonly tram-drivers but the last bit is poking fun at the fact they drink their beer warm.

33. If your mate has had a continuous run of bad luck, then he is likely:
    a. To *not* have killed a Chinaman in a previous life
    b. To shout all his mates to tea
    c. To chuck it all in *or* kill a Chinaman
    d. To chuck it all in *because* he reckons he must have killed a Chinaman

The correct answer is (d).

A continuous run of bad luck is attributed to variably having "kicked" or" killed" a Chinaman. I can not verify this but it probably relates to the gold rush era when their comparatively more modest claims yielded more gold than that of other prospectors'. Put differently, you would have Buckley's chance of making a brass razoo[13] next to a Chinaman.

34. Your mom asks you to come and have your tea. She is:
    a. Wanting your dinner not to get cold
    b. Wanting you back as she is about to pour your tea
    c. Asking you to shout
    d. Worried that you have forgotten to "slip, slop, and slap"

The correct answer is (a).

This one is rather close to my heart. Just two weeks in Australia my school friends invited me to "tea" in a Mexican restaurant. My mother promptly fed me a large meal and gave me a few dollars, enough to buy a cup of tea. We were both puzzled at teenagers being interested in tea!

It turns out "tea" is a meal, usually the evening or the biggest meal. I, needless to say, was quite embarrassed, so now it is my turn to get even!

The "slip, slop, slap" jingle was from a campaign against skin cancer. The aim was to encourage slipping on a shirt, slopping on sun screen, and slapping on a hat. To do otherwise would be to fry like a "silly sausage!"

35. Jacko asks you to "bugger off". He:
    a. Is inviting you to reconsider your original offer
    b. Is telling you furphies
    c. Cannot be a poofter
    d. Is on the wagon

---

[13] Small sum or virtually no money

*The correct answer is (**a**).*

We have already encountered "furphy" being a tall-story or a frank lie and also "bugger" in its strict sense. If someone asks you to "bugger off" they may be meaning to remove you promptly from the scene, as: "You had better bugger off before I ram my flamin' boot up your bloody arse." This is a serious and angry threat. You are well advised to comply with this request.

I, on the other hand, may say "bugger off!" to your offer of buying my car for a sum considerably less than what I had in mind. This is obviously the context in which the question was fashioned.

A "poofter" is a homosexual man. Use this term endearingly to any straight male friend thus: "G'day you big poof..." Be selective in using this term elsewhere as it does have a vulgar and politically incorrect connotation.

36. If you are calling Ralph on the big white phone, then:
    a. Ralph must live overseas
    b. You are driving the porcelain bus
    c. You are disinclined to use your mobile phone
    d. All of the above

*The correct answer is (**b**).*
This again is a reference to vomiting (See question 28).

37. Your mates say "come on, don't be a bloody poof, have one for the road". Then:
    a. You are being encouraged to date an ugly woman
    b. They have got wind that your old lady has summoned you home
    c. A delicious home cooked meal is out of the picture
    d. You are offered grog prior to departure

The correct answer is (d).

Your friends are encouraging you to drink before heading off on the road, an invitation you ought to resist if you are to avoid the boozbus[14]. The basis is to do with the colonial past. The criminal scheduled for a hanging would have been placed on a wagon and paraded through the town as a lesson to others. The public would have offered the criminal and the wagon-driver a drink: "Here, have one for the road!" The wagon-driver would have declined as he had to keep his wits about him. It would thus be said of him that he "was on the wagon." That is what a sober person or a tee-totaler is now known as.

I am having difficulty with the word "grog". I am lead to believe it is a reference to the sound a drink makes as it goes past the throat. It means an alcoholic beverage.

38. Which is *not* likely to be crook?
   a. A Queensland politician
   b. A Victorian cop
   c. A used car sales man from Parramatta
   d. The person who has been chased away from the hospital

The correct answer is (d).

The word "crook" variably means sick, twisted, or unsavory, and dishonest. The only person who is not crook is the person being chased from the hospital. If he was sick he would be getting treatment, we hope anyway! That is unless the hospital administration is crook.

---

[14] The boozbus is a Police vehicle fashioned as a mobile blood alcohol measuring station.

39. If you are fair dinkum about a deal, you are likely to be:
    a. Tentative
    b. In need of tax relief
    c. Unaware that the bloke is telling you furphies
    d. A kill joy.

The correct answer is (c).
To tell the truth is to be fair dinkum. A furphy is a lie. If you know someone is dishonest, it would be foolish to not play your cards close to your chest.

40. What is an attribute *not* associated with a jumbuck?
    a. A fleece
    b. Being jolly
    c. A billabong
    d. A Bunyip

The correct answer is (d).
The jumbuck is the sheep that the swagman encountered. It was near a billabong, it was jolly and had a fleece. Bunyip is the mysterious aboriginal beast that we encountered in question 20 and clearly is unrelated save for the legend holding the beast to loiter near billabongs.

41. BHP stands for:
    a. Bloody Horny Poofter
    b. Broken Hill Proprietary
    c. Bigger, Happier, Prettier
    d. Bendigo Harness Puller

The correct answer is (b).

This was also known as "the big Australian" and was a giant company mainly dealing with steel and petroleum. It is of course no longer.

42. If you are looking at a "dog's eye and dead horse", you are looking at:
    a. A potential meal
    b. An accident involving farm animals
    c. A woman with a disproportionately large buttocks
    d. A doorknob with a keyhole in the centre

The correct answer is (a).
Rhyming slangs are common. The "dog and bone" for example is a phone. Here the "dog's eye" is meat pie and "dead horse" is sauce. It is very Victorian and I am struggling to get New South Welshmen to accept it. My challenge is to have the non-believer go to MCG and leave this order with the canteen staff.

43. A "Uni bloke" is most likely:
    a. A gentleman living in the suburb of Unionville
    b. A student
    c. An employee of the Unilever company
    d. A workers' union representative

The correct answer is (b).
Uni is university and a uni bloke is a student. Witness what the foreman said to the developer when faced with opposition to the proposed road through a national forest: "If it weren't for them bloomin' uni blokes and the greenies we would have had the tractors in 'ere already."

44. It is half time at the MCG and you are purchasing a meat pie, which would the canteen attendant not offer you additionally?
    a. Sangas
    b. Snags
    c. Dunny door
    d. Dead horse

The correct answer is (c).

The Melbourne Cricket Ground is a famous sporting arena. You may well get sangas(sandwiches), snags(sausages), and meat-pies and sauce[15] but no one would offer you a toilet(dunny) door.

45. If your mate's old lady is a good sort, then:
    a. His mother is a kindly and pleasant lady
    b. His wife is pretty
    c. Both (a) and (b)
    d. Neither (a) nor (b)

The correct answer is (b).

A "good sort" is an attractive woman. Whilst "old lady" does occasionally get used to imply one's mother by and large it is applied to a wife.

46. If you have stolen a fag off your old man, then you are:
    a. Both poofters
    b. A poofter and he is not
    c. A bludger with an antisocial habit
    d. He is a poofter and you are not

The correct answer is (c).

---

[15] See question 42

In contrast to question 45, "your old man" is always your father. A woman will never refer to her husband in this manner. In this case you have "borrowed", "bludged", "pilfered" or otherwise obtained one of his cigarettes that were not intended for your consumption. This makes you a bludger with an antisocial habit!

A poofter(homosexual man) is not typically called a fag in Australia as an American might say. The alternatives were designed to confuse.

47. Of these, which is a common and very popular Australian snack?
    a. Scallops
    b. Dog and Bone
    c. A bush pig
    d. Jones's potato crisps

The correct answer is (a).

As you will recall, "dog's eyes and dead horse" is rhyming slang for "meat pie and sauce", as is "dog and bone" for "telephone". The latter term was intended to confuse.

A "bush pig" is an unflattering way to describe an unattractive woman and is clearly the wrong commodity to consume.

Potato crisps or chips for short come in a variety of flavors and makes. Smith's crisps are famous and popular but, as far as I can tell, there are no Jones's crisps!

Scallops are to a Queenslander what potato cakes are to other Aussies and really these are the only edible item available in the replies above.

48. Which of your attributes is likely to be compared to a dunny door?
    a. Your broad shoulders
    b. Your loud booming voice
    c. Your rude bits
    d. Your disproportionately large head

The correct answer is (b).

One could be said to be as loud as a dunny door, presumably a reference to the banging noise of the door when slammed harshly.

49. In Sydney, where will you *least* likely be able to find a wog?
    a. Cabramatta
    b. Parramatta
    c. Lakemba
    d. Watson's Bay

The correct answer is (d).

A wog, or a foreign-born Aussie, is likely to be found in all the above localities except Watson's Bay, home of the famous Doyle's restaurant. You would expect more "skipps" here. This term is as derogatory as wog but applied in reverse to local born Aussies and is a reference to Skippy the bush Kangaroo from the TV children's series.

50. If you have Buckley's chance of concluding a deal, you had better:
    a. Bugger off
    b. Crack onto the nearest Sheila
    c. Ask terms in writing
    d. Get heaps of grog to celebrate.

The correct answer is (a).

This relates to Buckley and his famous luck!

William Buckley was a convict transported to Australia who absconded from Port Phillip in 1803 and managed to survive in the bush when the aborigines confused him with a god. Another school of thought has it that "Buckleys & Nunn" was a store in Melbourne and "Nunn" rhymes with none. As in "no chance". Alternatively it is said that during the depression Mr. Buckley went to the bank and somehow managed to withdraw all of the "Buckleys & Nunn" assets before the bank ran out of money!

Regardless of the actual origin, if you have Buckley's chance of something happening your chances are indeed slim. You would be unlikely to want to celebrate by buying heaps of grog(beers). You may well want to drawn your sorrows but the reply specifically says the grog is intended to allow you to "celebrate".

You would in all probability want to salvage what you can of your dignity and leave. It would be ill-advised for you to randomly hit on(crack on) the nearest woman. Just take my word for it, bugger off!

51. In Melbourne if you "follow the footie", you most likely:
    a. Barrack for the Kings
    b. You are the goal keeper
    c. Barrack for Carlton
    d. You are a sanga

The correct answer is (c).

Carlton(or the Blues) is a football team in Melbourne.

To "follow the footie" is to barrack for one or more Australian Rules Football teams. You would not be barracking for Sydney Kings being a basket ball team.

A sanga is a sandwich!

52. Which of the following is not an exclamation:
    a. Streuth!
    b. Bugger!
    c. Flaming hell!
    d. Dunny!

The correct answer is (d).

"Struth" is probably condensation of "it is the truth" which to me sounds more like an explanation than exclamation but never mind that.

"Bugger" in this context implies surprise and is not to be taken literally. We had encountered this in the context of "buggering off" as in leaving hastily also. This is unflattering. It can be made magnified thus: "bugger me dead!"

If by now you still do not know what a dunny is I am clearly wasting my time. I had better bugger off!

53. If I ask you to take a "Capt'n Cook at my trouble and strife" you are *least* likely to say:
    a. Bugger!
    b. Chuck a left mate
    c. Crikey, you have done well!
    d. She is apples mate

The correct answer is (b).

More rhyming slang!

To "Capt'n Cook" is to look and your "trouble and strife" is your wife. Therefore, I am asking you to look at my wife. If she is particularly pretty you may say: "she is apples" or "bugger!" to register your surprise say at my good fortune. Equally if she is a bush pig you may equally be inclined to register your surprise, this time at my bad luck!

"Crickey" is yet another exclamation and has had a resurgence thanks to the late "Crocodile Hunter- Steve Irwin".

The one truly unrelated reply is the one dealing with turning to the left.

54. Which of these would *not* ordinarily be considered edible?
    a. A Chiko Roll
    b. Sangas
    c. Dogs eyes
    d. A cake-hole

The correct answer is (d).

A Chiko roll is a little like a spring roll and is quite tasty even if a little too fatty. Sangas are sandwiches and "dog's eyes" are rhyming slang for meat pie.

A cake hole or the moosh is your mouth, as in: "Do ya' wanna have me smack you across the cake-hole?!"

55. Jonsey is built like a brick shithouse, then Jonsey?
    a. Is an athletic sort
    b. Has a broad booming voice
    c. Likes his grog
    d. Has a poor constitution and likely to suffer regular fits of wheezing

The correct answer is (a).

The brick shithouse, the dunny, or an outside lavatory is a square construction that is typically hastily put together in wooden planks and inferior in workmanship; as in "Banging like a dunny door in the wind." However, the brick variety is stronger and the reference, I am told, is more to the square construction. A big burly bloke is said to be built like a brick shithouse, which is not commonly thought to be a derogatory remark.

> 56. Jacko has just told Davo, that Gazza has the hots for some Sheila. Davo is most likely to reply thus:
>   a. Bugger off!
>   b. Fair Dinkum?
>   c. She is apples mate!
>   d. All of the above

The correct answer is (d).

The question says that Jack has told David that Gary is admiring or is besotted by some lady. It requires you to select how David may respond to this piece of intelligence.

If the names sound funny it is because Aussie men like referring to their mates in this manner, a little like a pet-name. Such names are references to endearment and familiarity. You would only do this if you are good mates. Tim becomes Timo, Jack Jacko, Dave Davo and so on. Gazza however is Gary!

She is apples may mean that everything is alright. Imagine you have crashed your father's car and he says; "Righto. You are right. Then there are no worries. I will get the car sorted and it 'll be apples" He is actually saying: "Let us put things in perspective. You are unhurt. Then I am unperturbed. We will have the car seen to and it will be perfectly functional again." As is posed in this question, though, the phrase: "She is apples" means she is either pretty, or good natured or somehow or other possesses desirable traits. This is unlike the phrase "good sort" that always means only physically attractive. Davo may well say this if she is a catch.

In this context "bugger off" is not an invitation to make oneself scarce but more a phrase to register one's surprise or disbelief. In this sense the term is similar to the North American phrase: "get out of here!" For example she may have been out of his league, or Gary may have had a reputation as being a "poofter" or some similar disqualifier. "Fair dinkum" can be an exclamation, explanation, or question and is understood only by the facial gestures, tone and otherwise supra-semantic attributes of language. It probably comes from the Dutch and it actually means to be frank and truthful, on the level if you will.

57. Modesty aside, where would you *not* relieve yourself?
    a. In a dunny
    b. In a lavvy
    c. On a bunyip
    d. On the footpath in a back alley

The correct answer is (c).

By now you know that a dunny or a shithouse is a lavatory which was in the days gone by a term reserved for an outhouse but now applies to any lavatory. You should take note also that a lavatory is contracted to a "lavvy" to be able to answer this question.

In Australia, a "footpath" is the pedestrian section on the paved road known to the yanks as a "side-walk".

You may also recall that the bunyip is the mythical beast that loiters near watering holes. Go ahead pee on one. I dare you!

58. A snag is?
    a. A sandwich
    b. A rather thick sausage
    c. Not edible
    d. A man likely to frequent pubs

The correct answer is (b).

*Snags are thick Aussie sausages versus SNAG as an acronym for a **sensitive new age guy**. Whilst this acronym is used here I understand it to be an Americanism. Either way snags do not commonly go to pubs.*

59. A servo is?
   a. A slang word for Army service
   b. Where you buy petrol
   c. The same as a chunder
   d. A bull that has been put to stud

*The correct answer is (**b**).*

A servo is a service station. This is where you would buy petrol. You will not be served, in fact, as the vast majority of these outlets are self-service.

"Servo" rhymes with "berko", but this means to have a fight not a vomit.

60. If your best mate says of your sister that "she is apples!", which of the following best applies:
   a. It would have to be your shout then
   b. You are duty-bound to invite him to a jumbuck to preserve your family honor
   c. He must have been waltzing with Matilda
   d. You tell him he should have his eyes examined

*The correct answer is (**d**).*

As was canvassed in question 56, in the present context the saying implies that your friend has just said that your sister is attractive (or "a good sort"). You are unlikely to offer to buy him a beer ("shouting him grog") for such an utterance.

Matilda is actually a sleeping bag or a bed roll that the swagman carries and is clearly intended to confuse the uninitiated[16]. A jumbuck is a sheep and has nothing to do with jousting or any form of honor revenge.

It is clear therefore that true to the male Aussie form you would put yourself, your mate and your sister down!

61. Which of the following is a Western Australian?
   a. A sand groper
   b. A banana bender
   c. A Westie
   d. Lord Fleming

The correct answer is (a).

The title is unflattering but not vicious. It is a reference to the vast sandy landscape (and there is a lot of it). A banana bender means a Queenslander as a slight on the fact that they are more relaxed than the rest of us and have nothing better than bend bananas (which are already bent!)

A westie is a resident of the western suburbs of Sydney and is usually credited with the attributes of Shazza in question 2 and the man in question 7.

Lord Fleming of mouldy bread fame, the discoverer of Penicillin, was an English man!

62. I am trying to see to a clandestine liaison with my best friend's sister. A mutual friend sees us. What am I least likely to say:
   a. Bugger!
   b. Struth!
   c. Two shakes of a lamb's tail!
   d. Fair crack, mate!

The correct answer is (c).

---

[16] See question 6

In the present context "bugger" and "Struth" are both exclamations and are intended to display my displeasure at having been caught out.

"Two shakes of a lamb's tail" is a phrase one uses to ask someone's tolerance for a few minutes or excuse oneself from what one is doing to <u>briefly</u> attend to another task. I find the phrase enigmatic but the implication is probably brevity. Imagine you are on the phone and someone rings the door bell, you may well use this phrase to go and answer the door.

"A fair crack of the whip"- as it should be in full- refers to a stockman's attempt at getting his cattle or sheep rounded up. The crack of the whip should alone suffice to scare the beasts into orderliness and striking them is unfair. Here it is intended as appealing to the friend not to betray the secret.

63. I am flat out like a lizard drinking, then chances
    are I am a....
    - a. Busty woman
    - b. Man endowed with a beer gut
    - c. Busy person
    - d. Dole cheat

The correct answer is (c).

The term implies being busy the same way that an American may be "...busier than a one-legged man in a butt-kicking competition." It is a reference to the fast scooping of water onto the rolled tongue of the lizard.

64. What is a tucker box?
    - a. A slab of grog
    - b. Where you may stash your sangas
    - c. Not likely to be where your old lady puts your tea
    - d. A Wog chariot

The correct answer is (b).

Tucker is food and a tucker box is a place to put your food. Sangas being sandwiches are aptly placed there. A slab of grog[17] is too big to fit into an average sandwich box.

A wog chariot is a turbo-charged beast with fluffy dice or a heavy cross hanging from the rear view mirror!

65. Which of these is what you would look forward to after a hard day's work?
    a. A coldie
    b. A uee
    c. Pavement pizza
    d. A bogan

The correct answer is (a).

A "coldie" is a play on the word cold and is a reference to an ice-cold beer. One would not look forward to a U turn (uee), vomitus (pavement pizza), or a ruffian (bogan).

66. Where did the swagman alight :
    a. On the jumbuck
    b. In the billy tea
    c. Near the billabong
    d. In Cabramatta

The correct answer is (c).

The swagman rested near a cool billabong (brook).The jolly jumbuck was the sheep he found and billy tea is bush tea made by campfire.

Cabramatta is a neighborhood of Sydney that is mainly populated by the Vietnamese community.

---

[17] A slab contains 24 cans of beer

67. Fill in the missing words: "I love……..":
   a.   Aeroplane jelly
   b.   The Bonyip
   c.   Weet Bix
   d.   Cadbury

The correct answer is (a).
This was a TV commercial jingle.
Other than a bonyip, which is a mystical aboriginal animal, the other choices also define consumer products.

68. Who was the unlikely contender for the President of the proposed Australian Republic:
   a.   Jana Wendt
   b.   Tony Barber
   c.   The late Sir Joh
   d.   Eddie McGuire

The correct answer is (d).
Other than Sir Joh who was a Queensland politician of note, the remainder are either presenters or game show hosts. Sir Joh tried for prime minister in the 1980s but it was Eddie McGuire who actually tried his hand at running for president of the proposed Australian Republic.

69. Which is *not* a wog chariot in all likelihood?
   a.   BMW
   b.   Black Monaro
   c.   Falcon XB circa mid-late 1970s
   d.   A car with fluffy dice

The correct answer is (a).
As popular as they are with the Russian mafia, the average wog, would not drive a BMW. A wog chariot is typically a big powerful car or otherwise modified beast.

Fluffy dice or a big crucifix that hangs from the rear view mirror is mandatory.

70. If you are likened to a tramie, you are:
    a. Flat out
    b. Flat on your back
    c. Flat broke
    d. Being made fun of for being a bludger.

The correct answer is (d).

A Melbourne tram conductor (a tramie) is reputed to be lazy. You may well say of a loafer that he was "as busy as a tramie!"

On the other hand, one who is flat out, is busy, as elaborated in question 63.

71. Which do you *not* chuck:
    a. A wobbly
    b. A Uee
    c. A left
    d. A bandicoot

The correct answer is (d).

In replies to previous questions I have elaborated all manners of "chucking" but a bandicoot is a little marsupial that should not be chucked.

72. If you have had a Barney with your mate, then you are most likely to;
    a. Need a Maxillofacial Surgeon
    b. Be wet
    c. Have had a roll in the hay
    d. Have shared a meal

The correct answer is (a).

A barney is a scuffle or a fist fight and you will probably need your facial bones seen to!

73. What color was the Australian *one* dollar bill
    a. Purple and white
    b. Green and white
    c. Green and yellow
    d. Brown and white

The correct answer is (d).

Australia was, I believe, the first country to have her paper currency replaced by plastic (polymer) banknotes. The smallest denomination in polymer notes being a five dollar bill. There are no longer any one or two dollar bills in circulation. They are replaced by coins. The original paper dollar was brown and white and has not been, officially, legal tender for some twenty or so years.

74. The game involving the location of the security strip within the one dollar bill is called:
    a. Dollar dazzler
    b. Racing the Roos
    c. Blinky Bill
    d. Strip down

The correct answer is (b).

The paper dollar bill had kangaroos on the back of the note and these happened to be distanced differently in relation to the security strip. The game was to hold your dollar bill and that of a mate's to the light lined up exactly at the security strip. Whoever had the bill with the kangaroo forward would collect both bills. The term "roo" is short for kangaroo and the game was called "racing the roos."

75. Who was the chef featured in Healthy, Wealthy and Wise
    a. Belinda Roberts
    b. Ian Hewtson
    c. Rene Rivkin
    d. Jane Roberts

*The correct answer is (**b**).*
This was a life style show and the famous chef featured in it was Ian Hewtson. Rene is worth mentioning in that his "insider trading" efforts brought him and his empire into disrepute.

76. The Skipping Girl was the trade mark of what product?
    a. Gelatin Desert
    b. Ice cream
    c. Vinegar
    d. Olive oil

*The correct answer is (**c**).*
"Cornwell's Vinegar" established in 1895 has a skipping girl on its labels as its trademark.

77. Which of the following is a brand of matches?
    a. Strikers
    b. Red heads
    c. Sparkers
    d. Red Devils

*The correct answer is (**b**).*
It is interesting to note that the company is actually Swedish!

78. Which one is/was *not* a member of the ALP?
     a. Jeff Kennett
     b. John Cain
     c. Kim Beasley
     d. Paul Keating

The correct answer is (a).

Jeff Kennett was the Victorian premier and a Liberal party member. The other individuals were all Australian Labour Party members. John Cain was also a premier of Victoria who served in the 1980s. Kim Beasely was for a while Defence minister in the Hawke and Keating cabinets and then ran as shadow PM against John Howard and lost the election. He then had posts in the shadow cabinets under Mark Latham and ultimately resurfaced again to lead the shadow ministry.

79. Which is NOT an Australian Bird?
     a. Eastern Rosella
     b. Kookaburra
     c. Bird of Paradise
     d. Lyre Bird

The correct answer is (c).

"Bird of paradise" is any of various birds of the family Paradisaeidae. These are native to New Guinea and adjacent islands. They have brilliant plumage and long tail feathers in the male. All other birds are native Australian birds.

80. If a bloke says that he doesn't like birds, then
     a. He is most likely a pillow biter
     b. He prefers red meat
     c. He is a vegetarian
     d. He can't be a poof

*The correct answer is (**a**).*

A poofter or pillow-biter is a homosexual man and clearly he will have no inclinations towards a woman (a bird).The word "poof" is simply a contraction of "poofter". All these terms are vulgar and are not commonly used in polite company!

81. Which suburb in Melbourne is the equivalent of Sydney's Penrith?
    a. Caulfield
    b. Kew
    c. Bacchus Marsh
    d. Box Hill

*The correct answer is (**c**).*

This question warrants some knowledge of both Sydney and Melbourne. Penrith (pronounced by the natives as "Penrif") is an outer suburb populated mainly by battlers and Westies (bogans) same as Bacchus Marsh. Caulfield and Kew are uppity and Box Hill in Melbourne is a larger suburb probably like Hornsby in Sydney.

82. If you have just had a biffo, then which of the following is *not* true of you:
    a. You have had a barney
    b. An altercation has transpired
    c. You are a Sheila
    d. There has been a fist fight

*The correct answer is (**c**).*

A biffo is a fisty-fight or scuffle, also known as a barney. A woman (Sheila) may well fight but in the context of the question, "Sheila" is a noun meaning an effeminate man or a person who may abhor physical violence.

83. A ponce is a man who is:
     a. Effeminate
     b. Pretentious
     c. Built like a brick shithouse
     d. Dancing with Matilda

*The correct answer is (**a**).*

To be built like a brick shit house implies being very masculine, whereas a ponce is an effeminate man. A cuckold in its absolute and strict semantic sense is a man whose wife has a sexual liaison with another man. A pimp sells sexual favors of a woman for his personal financial advantage. A ponce, however, is a cuckold who pimps his own wife. The meaning has softened over the years to mean an effeminate man only.

Matilda is a sleeping bag and the reference is to the swagman by the billabong. The choice is intended to confuse the uninitiated.

84. If I have gone troppo, then I must be:
     a. On a pleasant vacation in the tropical north Queensland
     b. Apeshit
     c. Flat-out like a lizard drinking
     d. A flaming poof

*The correct answer is (**b**).*

"Troppo" is a contraction of "tropical" and refers to the heat of the tropics making one crazy or intolerant. If you go apeshit you are crazed or angered. In reply (d), the adjective "flaming" is to emphasize homosexuality (poofter).

To be flat-out[18] is to be busy and is unrelated.

---

[18] See question 63

85. With some personal risk you have managed to get a truckie to look up and say : "Waddya want, mate?" Your reply would be:
    a. Can I scab a lift mate?
    b. Ya reckon I can "pinch a fag off you?"
    c. Bugger off you big poof.
    d. You may reply (a) or (c) but never (b)

The correct answer is (a).

The word "truckie" is a contraction of "truck-driver" and truckies are over-worked, on a tight schedule, and notoriously short-fused. If you flag one down you are most likely to want to hitch a ride. You would have to be mad to go to the trouble only to ask him to "bugger off" which doubtless would lead to your need to attend the dentist. Equally you should avoid bumming a cigarette under the above circumstances.

86. If I reckon you can't take a trick, then I mean:
    a. You just can not accept a practical joke
    b. You are constantly unlucky
    c. It is your turn to spin in two-up
    d. You can not chuck a flamin' piss-up in a brewery

The correct answer is (b).

This implies bad luck at card games in particular and the reference to two-up is related but not an adequate explanation.

Inability to "throw a piss-up in a brewery" implies inadequacy or impotency.

87. If I call you a shark-baiter, then you must be:
    a. A Fisherman
    b. A raging poof
    c. A surfie
    d. From Townsville

The correct answer is (c).

*This is a clever albeit coarse reference to surfers being mulled by sharks. "Surfie" being a contraction of "surfer". A poof (poofter) is a homosexual man, referred to as a pillow-biter(**Vulgarism**). The choice was intended to confuse the uninitiated.*

88. If Davo gets his Sheila a prezzie, he can rightly expect to receive:
    a. A decent dunny
    b. A bit of pash
    c. A good bunyip on the side
    d. A jumbuck to kill for

*The correct answer is (**b**).*

Davo has just bought his woman a present and would be disappointed if he did not get some gratitude in form of sexual favors in return; "pash" being a contraction of "passion"! Strictly it refers to "necking" or foreplay but may be extrapolated to actual intercourse.

A dunny is a toilet. Unless Davo is a pervert a jumbuck (sheep) would not appeal and a bunyip- a mythical ogre-would clearly endanger his health.

89. You are expected to complete a task no matter
what the personal cost to you. Your task master is
likely to want you to persist even if it means you
must undertake:
    a. "Rogering the Duke of York"
    b. "Fighting a Joey"
    c. "Flogging a 100 poofs"
    d. "Taking a sickie"

The correct answer is (a).

*To roger (have intercourse) with the Duke of York is
likely to be a mean fete and implies personal risk at
achieving the task prescribed. A joey is a baby kangaroo
and you would not have too much difficulty fighting one.*

*If you are to complete a task you are not going to be
popular if you take sick leave and this is clearly the
wrong choice. Flogging of homosexual men, as choice (c)
implies, is also unrelated.*

90. You have just been done over by a grey ghost.
    You have;
    a. Been spooked by an old hag
    b. An old lady has cracked onto you
    c. Failed to chuck a wobbly
    d. The traffic warden has just booked you

The correct answer is (d).

*If you are "done-over", you have come off second
best in a contest or you have been somehow or other
abused or hurt.*

*To "crack onto someone" is to try and pick them up-
strictly speaking for sexual favors. The old lady (old hag)
reference is in relation to the gray hair and is aiming to
confuse. To chuck a wobbly is to be angered and this is
exactly how you **will** be if the traffic warden (the gray
ghost) has booked you. They wore gray uniforms and*

"ghost" is a reference to their stealth-full skill at getting you no matter how cleverly you park your car or how briefly you have let the park-meter expire.

91. A yabbo spins you a good yarn in the paddock, then it must be that:
    a. A dero has just told you a ferphie
    b. You are through shearing a Merino
    c. You have derived a good income from this year's wool harvest
    d. You came second best in a pub-brawl.

The correct answer is (a).

A yabbo is a down-and-outer and to tell a yarn is to tell a tall-tale, the reference being to spinning a yarn from cotton.

A ferphie is equally a tall-tale or a story tainted by half-truths.

92. A pig has just busted your chops, then:
    a. Chances are you are heading to a pub lunch
    b. Your old lady has finally decided to cook you tea
    c. The venue is the MCG and the Melbourne Hogs are the opposition
    d. By all indications you are back on the Ps mate

The correct answer is (d).

The pig is an unflattering term for a police officer who has just booked you ("busted your chops") and the presumption is therefore that you will be back on "P" plates to imply "Provisional Driver." There is no team called the "Melbourne hogs" as far as I can ascertain.

"Old lady" is an affectionate term for one's wife and much more rarely mother and if she has cooked tea, it would mean that she has prepared dinner for you. Again the response is entirely unrelated.

93. You have been arsed out, that is…":
    a. You have been selected to sing
    b. You have been sacked
    c. You are flat out
    d. You've gone troppo

The correct answer is (b).

This means being fired or dismissed and is the equivalent of being given the sack.

94. An alkie is most likely to be:
    a. All alone like a country dunny
    b. About to sink a duffer
    c. On the piss
    d. All of the above

The correct answer is (d).

"Alkie" is a contraction of "alcoholic" and he is probably drinking alone hence being all alone like an outhouse!

An unproductive mine is a duffer. If you sink a duffer you are going to bottom out. "Duffer" has been adopted to refer to an empty glass of beer, fancifully resembling a "dry-mine."

If you are on the piss; you are drinking. Beer, to be precise. The term is vulgar and compares the colour of beer to urine!

95. If I pay dirt on my mates, then I have had:
   a. No end to my bad luck
   b. My swansong
   c. A barney
   d. A biffo

The correct answer is (b).

To pay dirt is sometimes used to mean mud-slinging or defamatory remarks but the term actually means to achieve success and reach the object of one's search. It probably is a mining term, perhaps that your patch of dirt finally paid dividends. I am only guessing here, though.

One's swansong is oddly the song of success. It has nothing to do with how a swan is famed to sing a beautiful song before it dies. In that scenario a swan-song would be a tear-jerker, a vanquished or melancholy outcome. The modern "street" meaning of a swan song is to do with the TV commercial jingles of a few years back. It went something like: "They said you never make it,...[but you proved them wrong]" and thus you deserve a Swan beer. It would show a now-famous person like Ken Done getting knocked back at all turns. In case of Ken Done they would reject his painting and he would get rained on and so on. Ultimately though the last scene of the commercial would take you to his gallery, women hanging off him and he would be sipping Swan beer. That is "paying-dirt", or having your "swan song".

A biffo or barny meaning a scuffle has no relevance.

96. A perve is a term describing what?
   a. A lecherous man
   b. A nerd
   c. A dero
   d. A swag

The correct answer is (a).

"Perve" is contraction of the noun "pervert" to mean a lecherous man.

A dero is a down-and-outer and a swag is a bag or backpack that a wanderer may put his belongings into. These options were included as "window dressing."

97. You have just chucked a sickie:
    a. It must be Monday
    b. You are a gray-ghost
    c. You are dispassionate about what the day's footie match may be
    d. It would be unbecoming to refer to you as a bludger

The correct answer is (a).

To chuck a sickie is to request sick leave without being justifiably entitled. A Monday or Friday is a good choice for a day off as it can mean a long weekend.

"Sickie" is a contraction of "sick leave" but is "chucked" not applied for!

A grey ghost is a traffic warden and they are notorious for being as straight as an arrow and unlikely to fraudulently claim sickness benefits.

A bludger is a lazy good-for-nothing loafer and naturally apt to chuck sickies. Lastly the sickie is usually spent at the footie matches or on the beach.

98. A salvo is likely to:
    a. Make your headache go away
    b. Be superior to Bex powder
    c. Ask you for donations
    d. All of the above

The correct answer is (c).

A "salvo" is a contraction of the "Salvation Army" and they need donations to be able to run their service. The question is trying to get you to imagine salvo is some manner of an analgesic like "Aspro".

Bex powder was a popular APC pain-reliever composed of aspirin, phenacetin, caffeine (or some say codeine). The housewife may have taken a Bex and had a lie down for a whole host of ailments, real or imagined. Unfortunately the caffeine (or codeine) would cause an addiction to the medicine that ultimately lead to many cases of analgesic nephropathy and renal failure in the 1960s and 70s due to the carcinogenic action of phenacetin.

99. If I shout you a schooner of grog in Sydney am I likely to be more endeared to you than if I bought you a pot in Melbourne?
     a. Yes, because I just bought an extra 5 oz of beer
     b. No, because I short changed you 5 oz of beer
     c. The schooner in NSW is of equal volume to a pot in Victoria. I must like you the same
     d. Yes, because I bought you an additional 7 oz of beer

The correct answer is (a).

You must remember that to shout is to treat a person to (typically) a drink of beer. Grog is beer or broadly any alcoholic drink.

Both schooner and pot are measures of beer which are regulated everywhere except in Western Australia. There is another measure called a middy that the question does not introduce at all.

The question asks for a knowledge of the capacity of each glass measure and assumes you know Melbourne is the capital of Victoria and Sydney the capital of New South Wales. In Victoria and Queensland a pot will buy 10oz and oddly a schooner will buy 15oz in New South Wales and 9 oz in South Australia, elsewhere it is not regulated. A middy in New South Wales buys 10 oz and 7 oz in Western Australia. Confused? Well then let me tell you there is yet another (now defunct) measure called a "butcher" and was quite small so that the butcher returning to work after his pub lunch would not hurt himself! I can not find its actual volumetric attributes anywhere.

Put easily, a schooner in New South Wales is the most beer and in South Australia least, whereas pots and middies are similar having a volume roughly about 10 oz.

100. I have set up a naughty tonight, chances are:
    a.   I get a score between the posts
    b.   I am heading to a Pub in Parkville
         (Melbourne University)
    c.   A scone and cream is likely
    d.   None of the above apply

*The correct answer is (**a**).*

*A naughty is sexual intercourse. To get one in between the posts is a reference to scoring a goal in football (**Vulgar**) which is likened to sexual penetration.*

Naughton's is a pub in Parkville where Melbourne University is situated and is affectionately called "Naughties".

101. If someone refers to a mate as a cobber, then he is:
    a. A dike
    b. A chum
    c. A bum
    d. A Native of Brisbane

The correct answer is (b).

"Cobber" is an older term of endearment mainly used between two men. A teenager will not even know this term in all likelihood. A dike is a lesbian and will not in all likelihood use this term to describe the object of her affection.

A native of Brisbane is a Queenslander and thus a "Banana bender".

102. A synonym for a *Black stump* is:
    a. Back of Burke
    b. Dog on a tucker box
    c. Back of Beyond
    d. Both (a) and (c)

The correct answer is (d).

Both back of beyond and back of Burke mean as far from civilization as one can get and mean the same as black stump. There are properties named the "Black Stump", even a steakhouse, but they are probably just utilizing the currency of the expression, which is simply an imaginary outpost.

A tucker box is a container in which to carry one's lunch, a lunch box. The origin of dog on the tucker box is mysterious but almost certainly ties in with early pioneers who set out to explore west from Sydney. In the Gundagai district stands a monument to the famed dog, which sat guarding his master's rations and perished in the process.

103.A Box is:
    a. A sheep's pen
    b. Same as a dog's breakfast
    c. Scattered artifacts
    d. All of the above

*The correct answer is (**a**).*
Scattered artifacts or a messy place is likened to dog's breakfast.

104.Bikkies means:
    a. Biscuits
    b. Scones
    c. Money
    d. Both (a) and (c)

*The correct answer is (**d**).*
Biscuits, are cookies to Americans and the same way that money is likened to "dough" by them, bikkies are applied as monetary currency here.
Scones are small un-sweetened cakes made of flour and milk and served with butter, jam, and cream.

105.If you go to the "B & S", then you are most likely to:
    a. Be shopping for groceries
    b. Be looking for a shag
    c. Have your car broken down
    d. Be a Kiwi

*The correct answer is (**b**).*
This stands for Bachelors' and Spinsters' ball and was initially a novel idea for the folk outback to meet particularly given the vast expanses that sometimes separated two adjacent properties. Recently such balls have become commonplace even in major cities for the

thirty-something professionals. As a sign of times, they are no longer noble efforts either and may occasionally even be sleazy outings. This makes it possible to look for a quick "shag", or in other words sexual intercourse.

A kiwi is a native of New Zealand, being a reference to the flightless bird, the Kiwi, that lives there.

106.You have been called a *battler*, then:
   a. You must be a dole bludger
   b. You are making piss poor wages
   c. You are rolling in dough
   d. You have bikkies and tea

The correct answer is (b).

The term "battler" is not flattering but is always used affectionately and with reflection. It literally means one who toils hard to eke out a meager existence (but not prepared to accept hand outs). In stark contrast a dole bludger is one who despite being perfectly fit and able bodied chooses to subsist on social security rations, clearly an abomination.

"Bikkies and tea" are "cookies dipped in tea" and is a favorite of toothless oldies. "Bikkie" is colloquially used to mean money, as is "dough" to an American. It may be that a battler could only afford biscuits and tea but option (b) more precisely applies.

107.Someone reckons you are a bastard, then:
   a. You must have been born out of wedlock
   b. You are cunning
   c. He must be your mate
   d. All of the above

The correct answer is (d).

The term and all its implications are universal in the English speaking world but is applied with such eloquence in this country that most visitors take this colloquialism as being uniquely Australian.

One further comment is worth making. The term is not always derogatory as in "You lucky bastard!", "Jack is such a cunning bastard", "That bastard's horse pulled ahead just at the finish mark!"

108.Danno is a banana bender, then he must:
    a. Be from cane toad county
    b. Work in a plantation
    c. Be a flamin' poof
    d. Be a wanker

The correct answer is (a).

We have encountered "banana bender" meaning a Queenslander before this question. "Cane toad county" is yet another euphemism for Queensland pertaining to the large number of toads that roam this state having flourished without any natural predators in Australia.

Danno (a contraction of "Daniel") of course is not physically bending bananas nor does he have to be a plantation worker, he could for all we know be a physician or a barber. These references are simply to frustrate random guessing.

A wanker is one who masturbates (the purest usage of the term) but really is intended to mean a fool or an odd fellow.

A poofter is a homosexual man. Both latter terms are vulgarities and should be used with caution.

109. If you take your ankle biter to the aerial ping
     pong, then
     a. You have taken your dog to the park for a
         game of fetch
     b. You have taken your tike to the footy
     c. You have taken your wife/girlfriend to a
         beach volleyball match
     d. You are having sex

The correct answer is (b).

An "ankle-bitter" is a child. Witness the clever imagery as an implication of the height of the infant. Tike is another term meaning a child but its origin is obscure to me.

Aerial ping-pong is footy (football), very often applied to Aussie Rules, specifically.

110. If you have been called a Septic Tank, then you:
     a. Were not born in the lucky country
     b. Are probably a politician
     c. Are a sand groper
     d. Are endowed with a big belly

The correct answer is (a).

A septic tank is actually a sewerage receptacle but in this respect is rhyming slang for "Yank" which in it self is a contraction of "Yankee" meaning an American. It is not really flattering but not meant to be a slight on the Americans either.

If a "septic tank" is an American then he could not have been born in "the lucky country" (Australia).

A sand groper is a Western Australian, pertaining to the vast amounts of sandy desert in this part of the nation.

111. If you can not "chuck a piss-up in a brewery" you are:
   a. One to sink a duffer
   b. Unable to have a shag in a whorehouse
   c. As good as tits on a bull
   d. All of the above

The correct answer is (d).

The term implies inability or impotence. If you can not arrange a drinking session in a brewery or have intercourse in a house of ill-repute, you would have to be inefficient indeed.

"To sink a duffer" is to be unlucky in the strict sense but is extrapolated in general usage to mean being useless or ineffective. This is a mining term and was intended to mean much effort at sinking a mine shaft for it to produce no material gain. The author has also seen the verbiage used to mean a "drink". One may well presume that the reference is made to an empty beer glass. Witness the statement: "Gazza and I were just sinking a few duffers at the pub when Bill's old lady rocked up." Here the context is entirely different and is meant to mean that "Gary and I were in the pub drinking when Bill's wife chanced upon us."

Seeing you can not milk a bull having tits is entirely useless and implies the same as ineptitude.

112. If you are dealing with an Avo this Arvo, then you :
   a. Are probably making guacamole for a party tonight
   b. Are dealing with a person of Eastern European descent
   c. Are dealing with a person of Italian heritage
   d. Are sleeping all day

The correct answer is (a).

"Avo" is a contraction of "avocado" and "arvo" is similarly a diminutive for "afternoon". Therefore, if you are dealing with an avocado this afternoon, you are probably making a guacamole dip for the party tonight!

The Eastern European and Italian migrants are "wogs" and I know of no term to describe sleeping all day other than a "lazy bastard"!

113. Johno has just bailed Mick up, then:
    a. John has paid for Michael's release from Jail
    b. John has lied for Michael
    c. Michael and John are flaming homos
    d. Michael is getting an ear-bashing

The correct answer is (d).

In the present scenario, you are asked to determine what it means for John to "bail Michael up."

A bail up is actually a reference to how a sheep-dog may round up the flock, corner them and keep up the nuisance. It has nothing to do with posting a bond to free someone from the Remand Center. On the other hand, "ear bashing" is a euphemism for a person being subjected to a constant stream of verbal abuse, unsolicited advice, or gossip he does not necessarily care for. This is compared to a "bail up".

A "Homo" is a homosexual man(a contraction)(Vulgar).

114. A bastard on father's day, will most likely be:
    a. Drinking with the flies
    b. As happy as Larry
    c. Off to the party
    d. The first cab off the rank

The correct answer is (a).

In the present context "the bastard"[19] is a child born out of wedlock and the expression "all alone as a bastard on father's day!" has been coined to imply being lonely and unwanted. A similar expression is "drinking with flies" meaning that no one would be about in the pub and you have to keep company with the flies!

"As happy as Larry" is an expression of utter joy and is not uniquely Australian. Clearly our person is unlikely to be very happy and thus choice (b) does not apply. Equally if he has been reduced to drinking with the flies he has not been invited to any parties.

The implication inherent in the phrase "first cab off the rank" is one of speed or haste and clearly is irrelevant in the present situation.

115. Sharon just had a bingle, then
    a. She just had sex
    b. She was unfaithful to her husband or boyfriend
    c. She had a homosexual relationship
    d. She had a motor car accident

The correct answer is (d).

A bingle is a car crash and has nothing to do with sexual intercourse what so ever, unless of course that is what distracted Sharon!

116. What are bush oysters?
    a. Nasal mucus
    b. Witchetty Grubs
    c. Sheep's testicles
    d. Yabbies

---

[19] See also question 107

The correct answer is (a).

This is a comparison drawn between nasal discharge and oysters based on the similarity of consistency.

Witchetty grubs are the larvae of moths and beetles and are considered something of a delicacy by the Australian natives. The Grubs may be up to 15cm long and are eaten raw or cooked. They are said to taste like scrambled eggs.

Yabbies are fresh water crustaceans which whilst tiny are quite tasty.

117. Which is the odd term out?
    a. Donger
    b. Doodle
    c. Bitzer
    d. Old fella

The correct answer is (c).

These are all vulgar terms to describe the penis other than "bitzer". "Bitzer" is a contraction of "bits and pieces" and although a man may refer to his penis as his "bit", the term does not usually imply the penis. It refers to a hastily put together contraption with parts cannibalized from mismatching appliances. This is why the term is extrapolated to a mongrel dog of no pedigree also.

A doodle is an aimless drawing not often resembling a true shape at all. The origin is from a 17th century noun denoting a fool probably, in turn, from a German word "dudletopf" meaning an idiot or a simpleton.

The teacher may complain to a child's mother: "Johnny always doodles on the margin of the test paper." I have heard "doodle" applied to the penis but it is less popular than say "donger". "Old fella" meaning an old fellow is a reference to the penis in the flaccid state, implying creases and lack of employment!

118. Mappa Tazzie is a reference to
   a. A map of Tasmania
   b. The box
   c. Both (a) and (b)
   d. Neither (a) nor (b)

The correct answer is (c).

"Mappa Tazzie" is a contraction of "the map of Tasmania". The map happens to be triangular in shape and is likened to the female pubic hair distribution in the natural state. The word "box" is a vulgarity and is not used outside an all-male circle and even then is considered coarse. It means by definition the vagina proper and not just the pubic hair. Nevertheless the term is aptly applicable.

119. If your Bush Telly is Cactus, then
   a. Your television is on the fritz
   b. Your campfire is dead
   c. Your Boss is angry at you and it *is* your fault
   d. You are knocking a journo

The correct answer is (b).

When something is cactus, it is busted or damaged, broken if you will. The "bush telly" is a contraction of the "bush television" and is variably applied to the stars or the camp fire. The implication either way is the camper or swagman being so far in isolation that all he has got to entertain himself with is watching the night sky or the campfire.

To "knock someone" is to name call or take the "piss out of that person". This is tantamount to ridicule or defamation. A "journo" is a "journalist" for short.

120. Davo is giving the Aussie Salute,
    a. He is an ANZAC
    b. The blowies are about to make him spit the dummy
    c. He just relieved himself of some gas
    d. He just made a rude gesture involving his middle finger

The correct answer is (b).

As far as I can ascertain the official salute of an ANZAC (a member of the Australian and New Zealand Army Corps) is no different to that of a British military man but is dissimilar to an American soldier's. This is not the intent of the question.

The "Aussie salute" is a brilliant play on the fact that blow flies in the outback are extremely persistent and can be very annoying. The wave of the hand to brush away the flies is likened to a salute and clearly has no military significance. If you were to "spit the dummy" you are being angered over something otherwise mildly annoying- a childish anger. The spitting of the dummy (pacifier) by an infant typically follows tears of disdain. In daily usage though, "spitting the dummy is extrapolated to mean any anger, justified or otherwise.

121. Your mate has just had a bundy and coke, then he:
    a. Is probably injured
    b. Is probably high
    c. Is on the piss
    d. Is probably arrested

The correct answer is (c).

A "bundy and coke" is a mixed drink made of Bundaberg rum and Coca Cola. Bundaberg in Queensland is a sugar cane growing area and of course consequently has available the right commodity to make rum! The town itself is also called affectionately "Bundy" as in: "This avo I will be in Bundy but tomorrow I am back in Brisy!" to mean, "This afternoon I am in Bundaberg but tomorrow I will be back in Brisbane."

To "be on the piss" is a vulgar descriptor for drinking and probably is intended actually to imply beer given the similarity of its color to urine. Another possibility is probably related to the diuretic effect of alcohol increasing one's urgency for urination.

122. If you would not even "shout in a shark attack",
   then you are
   a. Rather reserved
   b. Not one to make fuss
   c. As tight as a fish's arse
   d. Quietly spoken

The correct answer is (c).

This is extremely clever. To "shout" is being implied in its purest form; that is to raise alarm- as the vignette would have it - in a shark attack. However "shout" is also to buy rounds of drinks for others, as we have seen before, say in question 99.

You are honor-bound to fulfill this responsibility when it is your turn to do so. If you are stingy-or a "tight-arse"-then you are not likely to "shout" when it is your turn to buy the drinks. The extent to which you are thrifty with money is likened to being as "tight as a fish's arse", really tight!

123. Mario is holding an item that is Clayton's, then
   a. Mario just got cheated
   b. Mario is a thief
   c. Mario lives in the bush
   d. Mario is probably a doctor or a dentist

*The correct answer is (**a**).*

Claytons were makers of a cordial marketed under the catch cry: "A drink you have when you do not want to have a drink!" The significance is one of abstinence from alcohol. It has since taken on the connotation that if something is Clayton's it is not the genuine article, or of questionable workmanship.

124. What does one most probably do with a durry?
    a. Drink it
    b. Smoke it
    c. Beat it
    d. Ignore him/her

*The correct answer is (**b**).*

A durry is a cigarette, especially a roll-your-own cigarette. Such a cigarette is one where you have to put tobacco in the cigarette paper and roll.

I have had old codgers[20] saying that a durry does not so much mean a cigarette, as a cigarette butt. They reckon that during the depression if you had not had enough time to finish your cigarette you would not chuck it away, instead you would extinguish it and put it in your pocket to smoke later. These half-smoked cigarettes, they said, were called durries.

The Macquarie Dictionary suggests durry may have come from a brand of roll-your-own tobacco called Bull Durham, and the "Durham" part being shortened to durry.

---

[20] A codger is a typically grumpy old grandfather figure. A crusty old fellow taken to complaining.

125.If you are Figjam, then you are,
    a. All over the place, not well put together
    b. A lesbian
    c. A fruitcake
    d. Up your own arse

The correct answer is (d).

*"Figjam" is an acronym for "fuck **I** am **g**ood, **j**ust **a**sk **m**e!" and is applicable to a person who thinks very highly of oneself, self absorbed. Such an individual is to be said to be "up one's arse" or less crudely, "up oneself". Both expressions are vulgar but the acronym has softened through usage and whereas most people know its implications not too many folks realize what it actually stands for.*

The reference to fruit cake or lesbianism is simply to confound the reader.

Response (a) is aiming to suggest looseness of the jam to mean hap hazard-ness and is not a correct response.

126.It's London to a brick that it will be a goer,
    therefore:
    a. You can go home and forget about it
    b. It may or may not happen
    c. It will certainly happen
    d. It probably won't happen but there is a slim chance

The correct answer is (c).

Something that is a "goer" is an event likely to transpire. That is indications are that it will happen but not necessarily immediately. As in "The wages increase is a goer but not 'til next Christmas."

If something is "London to a brick" it is precisely what it purports to be. In daily usage, though, it is taken to emphasize a proposition as if it were an adjective.

It is simple to assume that the expression probably meant that down to the last brick the presumed place resembles the city of London.

Thus if it is London to a brick that the event is a goer it is a "dead cert"[21] that it will happen!

127. Where will the publican serve you a smaller schooner than the one you are entitled to in Sydney?
    a. Brisbane
    b. Adelaide
    c. A schooner is a schooner always the same size
    d. At a servo

The correct answer is (b).

You will need to return to question 99 and revise the measures.

You also need to appreciate that Adelaide is the capital of South Australia where a schooner is 9 oz of beer and in Sydney (New South Wales) you are entitled by law to 15 oz of the "amber nectar."[22] That said, response (c) is clearly nonsense.

A servo is a service station and where you would take petrol for your car. In this nation they are not licenced to sell beer and even if they were it would not be poured from the tap as a publican would.

---

[21] "Dead cert" is a contraction of "dead certainty" and means it is a definite event.
[22] Amber nectar is beer.

128. If something is Shonky, then it is
    a. Dodgy
    b. Teed-up
    c. Bonzer
    d. OK

The correct answer is (a).

Something shonky is something or someone unreliable, dishonest, or crooked. The sort of adjective that may aptly describe a used car salesman!

The origin of the word is quite sinister however. Early in the 20th century the word "shoniker" was an anti-Semitic vulgarism to refer to a Jew; shoniker in Yiddish being a petty salesman or a peddler. It got contracted to "shonk" and that to which it pertained "shonky". In the modern sense the word is quite distanced from its anti-Semitic origin and until I did the research on the word I had no idea of its sinister origins.

On the other hand something "bonzer" or "bonza" is excellent. You may be a "bonza bloke" if you own a brewery for example. Its origin is a lot more innocent and probably from the diggers that came into contact with the French in WW I and copied "bon"!

Lastly, "teed-up" is a term borrowed from golf tantamount to teeing up a shot and means to plan an event, like: "I will tee-up a meeting but you are gonna have to ask the question yourself, mate!"

129. If you are walking to the pub and it is 20 clicks away, then:
    a. You can walk to it in a minute
    b. Chances are you will not be on the piss, any time soon
    c. You have already drunk too much
    d. You have your wife or girlfriend with you

The correct answer is (b).

A "click" is roughly a kilometer. Twenty clicks puts you away from the pub some 20 km and thus you will not be drinking any time soon.

The word "piss" is a vulgar term to refer to beer specifically (probably due to its color resembling urine) and all intoxicating liquors generally. It may also be that the diuretic effect of alcohol and its tendency to make you urinate, is being compared to "piss".

130. Which of these can you completely empty a full stubby into?
     a. A Pot glass in Queensland
     b. A Western Australian Middy glass
     c. A thimble in Adelaide
     d. All of the above

The correct answer is (a).

A pot glass accepts 10 oz but as we have seen already a Western Australian middy has a volumetric capacity of 7 oz. A stubby has 10 oz of beer.

131. To take a "squizz" is to take a
     a. Leak
     b. Capitan Cook
     c. Whack
     d. Sip

The correct answer is (b).

To take a "squizz" at something is to take a look at something. "Capt'n Cook" is rhyming slang for "look" meaning the same thing.

*To take "a leak" is to urinate and to take "a whack" is to have a go or an attempt at something but is applied to masturbation also implying forcefully striking the penis (**Vulgar**), like: "Whack off!"*

*As a noun it means to strike a resounding blow, as in:
"The blooming thing made such a whack it would wake
the dead."*

*I have seen the verb form more commonly used in the
negative to mean something is not neat, orderly, or
appropriate. That is to say "out of whack."*

*A specified share or contribution towards something
can also be a "whack", as in "Come on mate; that is a
fair whack of money for this bomb of a car!" Here the
person is haggling over the price of a car, which he sees
as a "bomb", or a questionable car.*

132. If a game is being played at the MCG, then it
probably involves,
   a. Stumps
   b. Fairways and greens
   c. The same thing as at the Gabba
   d. Both (a) and (c)

The correct answer is (d).

*The MCG is the **M**elbourne **C**ricket **G**rounds and the
Gabba is the Queensland Cricket Association grounds at
Woollon**gabba**, a suburb of Brisbane. Cricket, of course,
involves stumps and not fairways and greens, which
pertain to Golf.*

133. A longneck is a
   a. Tallie
   b. Kindie
   c. Bird
   d. Lollie

The correct answer is (a).

*A long-necked bottle of beer as opposed to a stubby
is affectionately called a "tallie" which is a corruption of
the word "tall". "Kindie", in turn, is a contraction of the*

German word kindergarten and lollies are sweets or candy.

134.If you are boiling a billy, you are
   a. Getting your goat prepared to service the ewes
   b. Shearing goats
   c. You are urinating in the toilet standing up
   d. You are camping

The correct answer is (d).

There is no such thing as "boiling of the (billy) goat." I made the term up to confound and confuse the uninitiated. The idea was that if you "anger or excite" the billy-goat it may service the ewes in the paddock.

The gurgling sound made in the urinal was compared to the boiling of a pot and is also the wrong choice.

The reference is actually to camping and making bush tea by boiling the billy. The billy is a cylindrical container for storing liquids, usually having a close-fitting lid. The proper ones will have been enameled but in the bush any container for boiling water and making tea will do. The word is first recorded in this sense from 1840s but there are several different stories that claim to explain the origin of the term "billy". Some say it comes from the Aboriginal word billabong, which literally means "dead water" or a pond without any fresh tributaries to feed it. Billy may simply be Bill from contraction of the name William based on the claim that "bushies[23]*" gave personal names to their cooking utensils. The source may be the French expression "boeuf bouilli" Anglicized to billy or that billy is a variation on the Scottish dialect word "bally" which has been applied to a milk container.*

---

[23] An affectionate term for a person from the bush.

135. A dingo's breakfast is
    a. Nothing
    b. A big mess
    c. An infant
    d. A bunyip

The correct answer is (a).

A dog's breakfast is a big mess. The dingo's breakfast is nothing, a dingo just gets up and gets going. The term "dingo" is aboriginal for dog and is very wonton when applied to a human for the animal having a reputation for cowardice and treachery. The animal is said to have taken human infants before but there is doubt as to the nature of such claims.

A bunyip is a mythical animal not known to have ever existed.

136. A butcher in Adelaide is like a
    a. Plumber in Melbourne
    b. Middy in Sydney
    c. Brumby in Albury
    d. Boomer in Fremantle

The correct answer is (b).

A boomer is a large kangaroo but may be applied to anything large and notable. Fremantle being a largish Western Australian Baytown is unlikely to have too many such beasts. A brumby on the other hand is a wild, untamed horse and you are not likely to find any in Albury, which is a town on the New South Wales-Victoria border. Brumbies roam wild in the outback having been set free or escaped from domesticated herds.

To answer this question you need to have understood the explanation to question 99 in as much as both butchers and middies are measures of beer. A butcher was a considerably smaller volume (I can not source the actual volume) to allow safety for butchers back in the workplace having had a beer with their lunches.

137. Pertaining to Australia specifically, Leyland Brothers were makers of:
    a. Double-decker buses
    b. B grade documentaries
    c. A grade wines
    d. None of the above

The correct answer is (b).

The Leyland brothers were makers of documentaries the last of which I recall seeing in the early 1980s though it may have been a re-run. They made the remarkable first Australian East to West Crossing by 4WD vehicles in 1966. The expedition took 111 days to complete. In all, 6797 kilometers were traveled.

Leyland motors makes double-decker buses famously adorning London streets. I have seen these buses as far away as Tehran, in the 1970s.

138. You are likely to find school of the air at:
    a. A little farm in the middle of nowhere
    b. Kingsford Smith Aerodrome
    c. An open learning centre
    d. RAAF airbase

The correct answer is (a).

The School of the Air is an ingenious Australian invention utilizing two way radios to bring education to distant communities. The lesson would simply be transmitted over the airwaves to reach outlying regions of the nation.

Royal Australian Air Force airbases may well have "ground schools" for their pilots but they are probably not known as school of the air.

Charles Edward Kingsford Smith was a famous Australian aviator born on 9th February, 1897. He studied electrical engineering at University before joining the British RFC (Royal Flying Corps). He flew his first combat mission on July 13, 1917. After the war he made many record breaking flights in an aeroplane called the Southern Cross, most notably an England-Australia flight between June 25 and July 10, 1929. The Sydney International airport is named in his honor.

139. If you would not be dead for quids, then you are:
    a. Fit as a mallee bull
    b. Happy as Larry
    c. In the crapper
    d. Only (a) and (b) are correct

The correct answer is (d).

To "not be dead for quids" means that no amount of money will encourage you to die! This is the same as saying you are "as fit as a malee bull" or "as happy as Larry". In contrast "to be in the crapper" is to be in the shithouse and implies life is down the toilet; no real incentive to go on. The origin of both sayings is obscure. The mallee is a low growing bushy eucalypt but why the bull that fed on this vegetation should be any stronger is anybody's guess. Goodness only knows who "Larry" was or why he was so happy!

140. You are in Adelaide, then a *floater* is a:
    a. Meatpie in a plate of peas or gravy
    b. Row boat on the Yarra
    c. Plank of wood on the Murray
    d. Both (b) and (c) are correct

The correct answer is (a).

All references to boating or pieces of drift wood afloat on any of our rivers or their tributaries has been intended to confound. A floater is a meat pie in gravy or thick pea soup, pure and simple.

Yarra is a river in Melbourne and the mighty Murray quenches the Riverina district.

141. If you are drinking with the flies:
    a. You are outback
    b. You can not hope any one to shout you grog
    c. You are down in the dumps
    d. Some one has dumped on you

The correct answer is (b).

To be outback is to be in the bush and sure enough there are lots of flies here but the expression is not relevant. To be "dumped on" is to be abused or told off or brought to bear burdens (may be unfairly) of your shortfalls and again has nothing to do with what the question is posing.

If you are "drinking with the flies" you are all alone and have no mates. The flies are keeping you company and you have no hope of being offered a round of drinks (a shout). It is possible to be down in the dumps yet surrounded by mates who repeatedly shout you beer, so response (c) is not correct.

142. You have just referred to your sister's new boyfriend as a "flash Jack", then he:
    a. Is ostentatiously clad
    b. Is by your reckoning a flamin' nancy
    c. Has swaggering behavior
    d. All of the above

The correct answer is (d).

There is invariably a hint of jealousy when a man refers to another as a "flash Jack". Such a person has an air of confidence and self import-be it deserved or otherwise. He may well be ostentatious, and will most decidedly be displaying his wealth in a swaggering manner. A show off.

Strictly a "nancy-boy" or more fully a "purse-carrying nancy-boy" is a term used to describe an effeminate man. A red-blooded Aussie macho man may well refer to anyone who is a little more polished than himself, thus. The adjective "flaming" is an old-fashioned qualifier not particularly popular.

143. Which is the odd one out:
    a. Bikkies
    b. Green backs
    c. Quids
    d. The Aussie battler

The correct answer is (b).

The Australian dollar is known affectionately as the little Aussie battler along the same lines as the "battler" we encountered in question 106. A quid was a colloquial term for pre-decimal currency (pounds) and is in use in other English speaking countries. It is now loosely applied to Dollars. "Bikkies", being a contraction of "biscuits" is also a term for money in the same manner as "dough" means dollars to an American.

"Green-backs" are US Dollars and are thus the odd term out, all other monies being Australian legal tender.

144. If you are a fiz-gig, you are a:
    a. Police informer
    b. First fleeter
    c. Wog
    d. All of the above

*The correct answer is **(a)**.*

This term is not well known but has currency. A fiz-gig was initially a flirtatious woman and one may make parallels with the present usage of the term in the ease with which a "fiz-gig" may impart information.

A wog is a person of foreign extraction but specifically an Italian or Greek.

145. If you could "flog a flea across the paddock, go home to tea and then come back and still find him," then:
   a. You are as mad as a cut snake
   b. As stubborn as a mule
   c. You are flat out like a lizard drinking
   d. Your land is parched

*The correct answer is **(d)**.*

This is brilliant imagery for a very parched land, so much so that not even one blade of grass can serve to hide your tiny insect from being recognized. To go home to tea and return is simply to exaggerate even further by applying an extra dimension-that of time. Imagine you go off to have a sit down meal, come back and still find the flea across the paddock, then that calls for some serious lack of vegetations!

"To flog" in the present contest is a verb not a noun as was encountered in "flogging a cigarette" (or bumming, stealing) but to "flick" as a whip-lash.

To be "flat-out" is to be busy and "as cut as a mad snake" is to imply anger not lunacy.

146. If you are spoken to thus: " Who is robbing this coach" , then:
    a. You are accused of constant interruption
    b. You better have a good explanation
    c. You are polishing the porcelain bus
    d. The slammer awaits you

The correct answer is (a).

This is not strictly an Australianism. It is common currency in the entire English-speaking world and means you are being accused of interrupting or interfering with a task assigned to someone else. It is essentially a protest. Something like: "Who is in charge of this duty, you or me?"

The "slammer" is the jail and is probably a reference to the slamming sound of the heavy iron-grilled door as it shuts behind a criminal.

We have encountered the porcelain bus many times already, this being a reference to heaving with head over the toilet bowl. Apparently the Yanks[24] refer to it as "praying to the porcelain queen!" I am partial to the "porcelain bus" myself.

147. You and your old lady have a kiss and ride system, then:
    a. You are both perves
    b. Your wife keeps the car after she drops you off at the station
    c. She is a good sort
    d. You are a squatter

The correct answer is (b).

Very innocently, it must be that you and your old lady (your wife) own one car so she drives you to the train

---

[24] A Yank is an American. This being a contraction of "Yankee".

station, "kisses you off and rides away" to perform her other errands. This must have been the prelude to car-pooling!

A" perve" is a pervert (a contraction) and is playing on the "kiss and ride" notion as if it were something naughty.

A squatter is one to usurp another person's property by stealth and not by force. One day you leave to go away and when you come back someone has "squatted" there. It is actually harder to extricate a squatter than you may think. The reference here is to being poor and unable to afford another car but the choice is clearly inapt.

148. I hand you a kip, then you are:
    a. As mad as a hatter
    b. A chef in the Japanese restaurant
    c. The spinner
    d. Within your rights to king-hit me

The correct answer is (c).

The kip is a small flat piece of wood on which the two coins in the game of "two-up" are placed. The game was present since the earliest days of the New South Wales colony but was played most enthusiastically by Australian soldiers ("diggers") of the WW I campaign. If you have the kip then you are the "spinner" meaning that you are to throw the coins up in the air. The famous call is made: "Come in, spinner!" and the spinner makes his toss. The toss is generally required to be at least eight or ten feet high.

The term "as mad as a hatter" is a reference to the fact that the milners of old used to soak hat rims in mercury well-known to be a neurotoxin now. They were credited with lunacy as a consequence. The Mad Hatter of Lewis Carroll's "Alice in Wonderland" is a brilliant representation of this fact. Not withstanding, the mad *hatter has nothing to do with the kip and constitutes a wrong reply.*

A king hit is a decisive punch. The recipient of any blow even by an infant will claim this to have been a king hit. The reference to king or royalty is to emphasize the significance of the blow.

149. If something is Jerry-built then it is:
    a. Soundly manufactured
    b. Made in England
    c. A bloody lemon
    d. Not likely to be the Clayton version

The correct answer is (c).

Anything, which is jerry-built, is badly built or hastily assembled. It implies inferior workmanship, being shoddily and flimsily built. It is romantically claimed that the term took origin from the city of Jericho, remembering that Joshua's army was able to destroy the wall by blowing their trumpets.

More probably the term was popularized after Jerry someone or other made some terribly sub-optimal appliances.

The concept of a Clayton item has been covered in question 123, meaning a sub-optimal contraption along the same veins. A Jerry-built item is most decidedly Clayton's making the reply (d) wrong.

A lemon, mainly in reference to automobiles is also an inferior quality item.

150. A Wongi in Sydney is:
    a. A wog elsewhere
    b. A Chinaman in Albany
    c. A yarn
    d. Both (a) and (c)

The correct answer is (c).

A wongi is a friendly yarn. The term is not in common currency.

*The term wog had meant to stand for **Westernized Oriental Gentleman** and was never intended to be derogatory unlike the other term "chinaman" that initially was neither flattering nor defamatory but is now considered quite malicious.*

The choices (a) and (b) are both playing on the popularity of the Chinese name "Wong"- actually meaning gold - to frustrate any effort at guessing at the correct answer.

I have extensively covered "wog" before but for sake of posterity it should be said that a wog is today any foreign person but should be applied specifically to a Mediterranean person. For example a Vietnamese, by definition, is <u>not</u> a wog but is often still called so.

There is an alternative theory to the acronym offered above in that wog is a contraction of "golliwog". Golliwog was the name given to a black-faced doll in a series of children's books written by Bertha Upton. This may explain why Asian migrants are less likely than Arabs or Greeks to be called a wog[25].

151. If a walloper has done you over, then chances are:
    a. A more handsome man has stolen your wife
    b. You are spending the night in the remand centre
    c. Your money was on the wrong greyhound
    d. All of the above

The correct answer is (b).

---

[25] See also question 21.

A "wolloper" is a police officer. In fact to wallop is to strike or hit with a severe blow. It also implies a large size as in: "Mate! I got walloped by yet another bill from that crook bastard."

"Done over" is to be completely vanquished. It probably got its roots from cooking! Either way, in this context, the police constable has booked you for something significant and you are off to the remand center.

If a man runs off with your wife you are in fact "walloped" and indeed "done over" but the man is not a walloper unless your wife ran off with a cop.

152.A grunter is a:
    a. Hot rod
    b. Meal of beans and sausages
    c. Cheap harlot
    d. Trendy man taken to showing off

The correct answer is (c).

The "grunt" pertains to sounds of sexual intercourse and is a vulgarism. The remaining choices all play on the theme of the noise of a grunt. A "hot rod" is a souped up car and as the muffler is often sawn off, these beasts do make a ghastly noise and beans, of course, are the "musical fruit".

153.What is a "wood and water Joey?"
    a. A baby boomer just after he will leave his mother's pouch permanently
    b. A bloke who does the menial tasks at the station
    c. A person down in his luck
    d. A carpenter

The correct answer is (b).

A "Joey" is a baby kangaroo (boomer) but the term is applicable from birth to departing the pouch and not *after* the kangaroo permanently leaves-becomes a boomer in his own right. All that is, however, beside the point. A "wood and water Joey" is a station hand put to menial tasks such as gathering wood or fetching water ; a dog's body.

154.If you have been served up grouse tucker, you will be:
   a. Excused for having chucked a spaz attack
   b. Greatly satiated
   c. Needing a decent meal
   d. Doubtless having bikkies and tea

The correct answer is (b).

Something "grouse" is excellent, outstanding, or optimal. "Tucker" is any manner of food. If you are served "grouse tucker" you ought to be greatly satisfied and should no longer be seeking a decent meal (choice (c)). Such a meal is unlikely to have been Bikkies (biscuits) and tea, unless you have modest culinary demands.

A "spaz attack" is a "spastic attack" and is an unfortunate (and inapt) phrase based on the misunderstanding that spastic individuals, who have inability to control muscle coordination, are also necessarily dim-witted or uncoordinated, or thrown into fits of rage. This is offensive, be it a noun or adjective, and is really only in currency in school yards[26].

All said it should be obvious that having had a decent meal, you have no justification to complain of the serving.

---

[26] We had encountered this term in question 17 also.

155. A tomahawk is likely to get:
    a. The sack
    b. Promoted
    c. Your hair singed
    d. A Yank on your back

The correct answer is (a).

A tomahawk is a station-hand whose ineptitude for shearing sheep causes him to repeatedly nick the skin of the animal. A rough shearer, if you will. Such a person is likely to get the sack, or be dismissed.

To "get the sack" by way of dismissal probably comes from the old habit of tradesman carrying the tools of their trade in a bag. When the foreman hands you your sack of tools, or perhaps your tucker bag, you know you are "done for" (see also question 151).

The tomahawk is a battle-ax of the American Indians and is now a name given to a ballistic missile. The missile is unlikely to just singe your hair, and in the original meaning the battle-ax was for scalping not singeing. The reply is thus clearly wrong.

A "Yank" is a contraction of "Yankee" meaning an American. To have "someone on your back" is to have a person constantly pestering you, or telling you what to do. This again is inapplicable and was just to throw you into confusion with the parallelism between an American and a tomahawk.

156. What is a dumper?
    a. A privy
    b. That which assures a grouse wipe-out
    c. A pommy
    d. A police informer

The correct answer is (b).

A *"dumper"* is a significant wave that breaks and drags the surfer riding it down before it reaches the shore. The term is a surfing jargon much the same way as *"wipe out"*. *"Grouse"* is an adjective meaning excellent or outstanding.

As we saw in question 32, a *"pommy"* or *"pommie"* is a corruption of the acronym POHM standing for a **Prisoner of His** (**Her**) **Majesty** and refers to an Englishman; taking its root from the days Australia served as a convict colony. The term has nothing to do with surfing and I just chose it as a play on the word *"dump"* implying that the prisoners were off-loaded (dumped) here.

A vulgar term for defecation is to *"take a dump."* A privy is not, however, known as a dumper, the most common term for the latrine being a *"dunny"*.

The last option (d) was chosen based on the notion that a police informer would *"dump"* on someone but the reply is clearly incorrect. The notion of *"dumping on someone"* is to tell on him, abuse him verbally, or challenge him incessantly.

157. Which of the following is an occupation?
    a. Postie
    b. Milko
    c. Sparkie
    d. All of the above

*The correct answer is (**d**).*

A "postie" is a post-man, a "Milko", a milkman, and a "Sparkie" an electrician.

158. A forlorn hope of success is:
     a. Buckley's chance
     b. London to a brick
     c. A wiped cat's testicles
     d. Digger's rest

The correct answer is (a).

If something is "London to a brick" it is precisely what it purports to be meaning that down to the last brick the presumed place resembles the city of London. It is not the correct answer.

Buckley's chance is, as we have already encountered, the correct answer and probably reflects on Buckley's unusually lucky survival story.

A "digger" is a soldier, typically of low rank, and is a term of affection. It was probably coined in relation to digging of trenches in the WW I campaign. There are many places called "digger's rest" and all are cashing in on the notion of physical toil of the digger.

159. If you are as full as a goog, then you will be disinclined towards a:
     a. Home-prepared tea
     b. Smoko
     c. Bonza bloke
     d. Cracker of a Joke

The correct answer is (a).

A "goog" is a corruption of "egg" and if you are as full as a goog you will not want to eat anymore. It is a clever illustration of the limitation in available space within the confines of an egg. A "cracker of a joke" is a side-splitting joke. It cracks you up. It is not unbecoming of a satiated person.

A "smoko" is a contraction of smoking break and actually goes hand-in-hand with a lunch or coffee break in the work place.

Lastly, a "bonza" bloke is a nice guy and is unrelated to meals or a sense of fullness.

160. Your mate is out back for a *big spit*, then :
    a. He is having pavement pizza
    b. The dunny must have been available
    c. He must be a keen bush-walker
    d. He is likely to be made a lot more popular with the birds upon return

*The correct answer is (**a**).*

In this context "out back" is just away from the household and does not necessarily mean the wilderness. It could just be a corner of the backyard. The "outback" is a specific noun meaning the bush. Therefore, the reply pertaining to bush-walking is inappropriate (c).

The "big spit" is a vomit as is "pavement pizza" and no matter how uncouth a man may be if the privy (the dunny) is available he ought to use it. This makes choice (b) false.

In this context the term "bird" is a mildly derogatory but well-intentioned descriptor for a woman. Other than an extreme mysanderist a woman ought not to object to this term. That said I am yet to find women who find the spectacle of a drunken buffoon who has just vomited endearing, thus the last choice is also incorrect.

161. Johno is spitting chips, he is likely to be:
    a. Mulching the garden
    b. Blowing his stack
    c. Issuing forth a son
    d. Having a chunder in the dunny

The correct answer is (b).

To be "spitting chips" is a term to describe extreme anger. The analogy is to biting the trunk of a tree in your frustration and spitting the chips off. Steam-driven engines of the yesteryears had a safety valve to release the excess steam. If there was too much, the stack may have blown. The term has endured and means anger also.

The reference to the son is taken from the expression "a chip off the old block" to refer to an offspring that resembles in attitude or appearance his father.

To chunder is to vomit and is also known as the big spit but is unrelated to the present context.

162. If all is crook in Muswellbrook, then:
    a. You should not go apeshit
    b. You are as full as a boot
    c. You are well advised to get on your neddie
    d. Bob is your uncle

The correct answer is (c).

"Crook" means ill, unwell, or sick when applied thus: "I was crook yesterday but still finished the report." It can also mean shady, or underhanded when applied say to a politician or a used car salesman.

Muswellbrook is a little town and the phrase "all is crook in Muswellbrook" is a rhyme you would use to add emphasis to the unsavory circumstances you find yourself in. Under such circumstances you would do well to get on your proverbial horse (neddie) and get out! A "neddie" or "neddy" originated from the word a child might use to describe beasts of burden. The term is quite dated.

If you are "apeshit" you are rather miffed and upset, very angry if you will. The term is often shortened to just "ape" as in: "Come on mate! Don't go ape at me the bloody thing was cactus when I got here." Meaning that whatever the person is accused of having damaged is being claimed to have been broken already and there is no justification for the allegedly misplaced anger. In the present context seeing things are no good, you may well be apeshit. Thus reply (a) is not correct.

I have seen the expression "Bob is your uncle" used with impunity in Australia, Ireland, England, Wales, and Scotland. I am also told it is currency in South Africa and New Zealand. I have no clue as to how it came about but there is a story concerning Arthur Balfour (British Prime Minister) who achieved office based not on his merit but on the fact that his uncle was Lord Salisbury (named Robert). Therefore, if Bob is your uncle everything is ok whether you deserve the breaks you get or not. Thus you have no reason to want to leave, making reply (d) false.

"To be as full as a boot" means to be drunk, with inebriation being exaggerated to full capacity. The reply is irrelevant in the context of this question.

163. "Nannas" are:
    a. What Queensland is famous for
    b. A reference to retirement homes
    c. To be harvested in large numbers in Tasmania
    d. Both (a) and (b)

*The correct answer is (**a**).*

This question is admittedly quite mean. "Nanna" is a contraction of banana and Queensland is famous for bananas hence a Queenslander being a banana bender. Tasmania is too cold for banana plantations, making (c) wrong.

A child may refer to a grand mother as "nana" but the spelling is with one "n." A retirement home (that is "nana's" home as may be said by a child) is misleading and is not a correct reply.

164. You are discussing the "awnings over the toy shop" then you are likely to be:
    a. Contemplating the purchase of the business
    b. Taking the piss out of your mate
    c. A peeping tom
    d. Canvassing for a new job

The correct answer is (b).

This is actually quite cute but can be vulgar too. The "awning over the toy-shop" is how a middle-aged man may refer to his pot-belly. Secondary sexual characteristics in a man dictate re-distribution of fat to the abdominal region (compared to the hips in a woman). The "awning" being the sagging belly and the toy shop being the genitalia. Clearly all choices are wrong save for reply (b) in that to take the "piss out of somebody" is to jokingly annoy or abuse that person.

165. If I go crook at you, then I am
    a. Spitting chips
    b. Chucking a wobbly
    c. Likely to spit the dummy
    d. All of the above

The correct answer is (d).

Of the explanations canvassed for "crook" in question 162, the one pertaining to the present scenario was purposely left out. "Crook" can also mean angry, upset or disenchanted. All of the choices mean the same thing making reply (d) correct.

As seen in question 161, spitting chips is an indicator of extreme anger and probably implies biting the trunk of a tree in frustration and then spitting the chips off (At least if I say it often enough you may believe my theory)! Spitting the dummy(pacifier) is a child's way of showing disdain, as is "chucking a wobbly" which is more like throwing a tantrum.

166. A mollydooker is:
    a. A girl with a bad reputation
    b. A left handed person
    c. Out in the never-never
    d. One who has a roaring trade

The correct answer is (b).

I have no idea why a left-handed person is a "mollydooker" and no one has been able to enlighten me. My research has drawn all blanks but I have a theory - yes! Another. Supposing this is actually Molly Dooker and this person was a famous left handed woman then the term slowly got applied widely. The trouble is why this particular person, and how!

The "Never-never" is an affectionate mythical place comparable to the term "back of Burke" and really means far away from populated regions.

167. Your balls (gonads) can be aptly referred to as:
    a. Avos
    b. Acres
    c. Arvos
    d. Abos

The correct answer is (b).

"Arvo" is a contraction of "afternoon", as is "avo" a contraction of "avocado". "Abo" is the diminutive form of "Aboriginal" but is derogatory. I recommend you not using it. Your balls would ache if they were struck, making them "achers". "Acres" is just a corruption of the same word.

168.If you are knackered, you are
    a. Buggered
    b. Nana'ed
    c. Fit as a fiddle
    d. Laughing your arse off

*The correct answer is (**a**).*

If you are "knackered" you are very tired or buggered. A knacker was a slaughterer of horses, one who would dispose of beasts of burden that were no longer serviceable. It also became applicable to a castrator. Either way if you are knackered you are extremely tired, worn-out, over-worked or abused. In reverse to be as "fit as a fiddle" implies health and vigor and is not the correct response. There is another term "to fiddle while Rome burns" which means attaching significance to little things whilst ignoring the important matters and the two phrases may be related. The reference could also be to Nero setting Rome on fire and watching it burn for his perverted amusement. The idea is that he was not worried nor concerned. It implies restful detachment from events.

You "laugh your arse off" when you have something really funny to amuse you. If you are knackered you are probably not good humored.

169.What is likened to a cut snake?
    a. A month of Sundays
    b. A bloke who is short
    c. A woman who has accused her husband of indiscretion
    d. One who is as funny as a fart in a lift

*The correct answer is (**c**).*

The expression in full is "as mad as a cut snake" and we have encountered it before. Witness the wiggling and twists and turns a cut snake may do. This is likened to extreme anger. If a woman finds her husband to have been indiscrete, she is likely to be similarly tempered.

A month of Sundays is a joyous event but clearly impossible, however fabulous such a thing may be. This is why it is used often in the negative sense as in: "Not in a month of Sundays will I shout that bastard another beer", meaning the bloke to whom is being referred has Buckley's chance of getting a free beer.

As funny as a "fart in the lift (elevator)" is a sarcasm for something that is not at all amusing. It is going to upset but the response is not as appropriate as reply (c).

170.If I threaten to punch you in the moosh, then you:
    a. Had better nick off
    b. Would be a mollydooker
    c. Must be a pearler
    d. Are a good sport

The correct answer is (a).

One's "moosh" is his mouth, or his "cake-hole." Slop or porridge of the kind I was reduced to eating in the hospital during my training is also referred to as "moosh" or "mush." If I threaten to smack you across the moosh, I am not endearing myself to you and you had better leave ("nick-off") unless you want to have a biffo[27].

A mollydooker is a left-handed person and has nothing to do with this question. A "pearler" is a good or excellent version of anything but mainly said as: "Davo is a pearler of a bloke" which really means the same as a nice guy or a "good sport". Such a man should not enrage me to the extent that I would threaten to strike him.

---

[27] A biffo, or barney is a scuffle.

I do not know where the expression "pearler" actually came from but it may relate to the value of the gem itself.

171. If someone bangs like a bloody dunny door, that person has:
     a. A big spit
     b. Questionable moral standing
     c. Sloppy Joe
     d. A Shank's pony

The correct answer is (b).

As you know by now, a dunny (outhouse) is typically hastily assembled and of inferior construction and so it's door is said to bang loudly. Witness: "As loud as a dunny door" to mean a person has a strong voice, or "to bang like a dunny door in the storm" to mean noise mainly during sexual intercourse. The term is offensive but has been extrapolated further to mean a prostitute or a woman of lax moral standards.

If you have a "big spit" you are having a vomit.

Sloppy Joes are simply pull-overs (jumpers) typically a couple of sizes too big that fit loosely. The reference is to the sloppy or loose fit of the garment.

A "shank's pony", like sloppy Joe, is unrelated to the question and means a pedestrian. The reference is to your feet being a pony to your legs.

172. If I am a tat shirty, then chances are I am:
     a. Cruising for a good shag
     b. Aching for a biffo or barney
     c. Gonna get a flamin' good root
     d. Both (a) and (c) are correct

The correct answer is (b).

A "tat" or "tad" is a little of anything. To be "shirty" is to be angry and upset and probably pertains to the pulling and tugging men make at one another's shirts edging each other along before a frank scuffle ensues.

This is a long shot but the term "tat" or "tad" may be a contraction of "toddler" or "tadpole" to mean a small child and by extrapolation anything small. Either way to be a "tat shirty" is to be a little angry and aching for a barney or biffo[27].

To be "cruising", "dying", or "aching" for something is to want it badly. Reply (a) and (c) are both vulgarisms for sexual intercourse and do not relate to the question being canvassed.

173. If you are a couple of tinnies short of a slab, then:
    a. I wont shag you with my mate's donger
    b. You are a few snags shy of a barbie
    c. You are going twenty to the dozen
    d. You are likely to bang like a dunny door

The correct answer is (b).

A slab carries 24 cans of beer. A "tinnie" is a corruption of "tin" or "can" of any beverage. So if one is "a couple of tinnies shy of a slab" that person is implied not to be "whole", or in this context dim-witted. A "couple of snags shy of a barbie" is "a couple of sausages too short to have a barbeque" and means the same thing.

On the other hand "to go twenty to a dozen" is to be fast and furious or too much of something and is a wrong reply.

Albeit vulgar, I think the expression "not shagging someone with a mate's donger" is as clever as an expression can get. It means a girl is so ugly you are not even prepared to have sex with her even if you were using someone else's penis. That is much too ugly!

We have encountered reply (d) in question 171 already and that, of course, is inapplicable.

174. What is a dead cert?
   a. A bounced cheque
   b. A boomerang
   c. Sure thing
   d. A mortician

The correct answer is (c).

A "dead cert" is a contraction of "dead certainty" and means a sure thing. "Dead" can act as an adjective to bring about extra emphasis. As in: "Listen mate, I am dead sure it was your missus at the pub with Jack!"

The remaining replies were designed to frustrate guess work. A mortician may make you think of "death certificates" and a "bounced cheque" a "dead certificate"! A boomerang does not necessarily return unless you have thrown it well to begin with so is by no means a sure thing.

175. If you pull up stumps in a bloody hurry, you are:
   a. Off like a bride's undies
   b. Hitting the frog and toad
   c. Aptly comparable to a Bondi tram
   d. All of the above

The correct answer is (d).

The term "pull up stumps" is a reference to the game of cricket when at the end of a match stumps are removed. Therefore, to "pull up stumps in a bloody hurry" is to be rushed. "Off like a bride's undie[28]" means the same thing and implies the haste the groom may exercise in wanting to consummate the marriage.

---

[28] "Undie" is contraction of underwear.

The Bondi term is of course no longer but was famed to not stop all stations and be hard to catch; again emphasizing haste.

Whilst "to hit the frog and toad" does not actually imply haste, it does make reply (d) the most apt. The "frog and toad" is a rhyming slang for "road" and implies "hitting the road." That is departing.

176. Your plate of meat is called into action, you are getting:
    a. Pissed as a parrot
    b. By without your car
    c. A rudie
    d. Your laughing gear used with impunity

The correct answer is (b).

Your "plate of meat" is your feet (rhyming slang). If they are being used then you are not driving making reply (b) correct.

To be "as pissed as a parrot" is very drunk and is unrelated. The "laughing gear" is the same as mouth and unless you are prone to having your foot in your mouth, the reply is irrelevant.

A "rudie" is sexual intercourse and the implications are that it is something rude on the strength of Judo-Christian beliefs of inappropriateness of sexuality outside the sanctity of marriage. Again it does not apply to the question.

177. If you are getting a backroom waltz, then:
    a. You are regretting the Indian meal you consumed earlier
    b. You hadn't blown your brass on flowers and lollies
    c. Things are crook in Muswellbrook
    d. A dilly-bag is in order

The correct answer is (c).

"Backroom waltz" is the brand of justice that may be served in the cop shop[29] (unlawfully). If you are getting this brand of justice things are no good (crook).

A dillybag is a food bag and makes no sense in this context.

The Indian food you consumed earlier may well burn again the following morning but the backroom waltz is not the wriggles of abdominal discomfort!

Reply (b) is unrelated but interesting. The expression is used when you have no chance of winning a girl's favor your mates may say: "Do not blow your brass on flowers or lollies, she is taken (or some such reason)." The expression is inviting you to reconsider spending money (brass) on flowers and lollies (sweets) seeing your offerings are unlikely to win any favors.

178. Which does not pertain to a fart?
    a. To cut the dog in half
    b. A dead dingo's donger
    c. To Drop your guts
    d. Dutch oven

The correct answer is (b).

Dingo is a native dog. A dead dingo's penis (donger) is taken to symbolize dryness and is unrelated to a fart.

To "cut the dog in half" or to "drop one's guts" is to fart whilst "Dutch oven" is a game male Aussies (generally school aged!) play in farting under a bed spread that is being held over a friend's face!

---

[29] A cop shop is a police station.

179. A mystery bag, is:
   a. A sausage
   b. A prezzie
   c. Your surprise Easter show bag
   d. A blind date

The correct answer is (a).

A "mystery bag" is a sausage in that you have no idea what the butcher has put in it.

A "prezzie" is a "present" and may be mysterious but is the wrong reply to the present question.

The Royal Easter Show is a rural affair that is brought to the city where prized bulls or sheep are on display. There will be a pet judging contest, sweets for the kids and much fan fare. The Easter Show bag is a bag with goods from different manufacturers. For example Nestle may have all its chocolate samples in a bag for sale. There may be toys and other paraphernalia. Generally though, the contents are never a mystery to the kids!

180. Your missus has just gone crook at you:
   a. Your wife is unwell
   b. She just found lippie on your collar
   c. You will surely get a leg over
   d. None of the above

The correct answer is (b).

We have seen "crook" in all its meanings before. Here it is to mean "angered", "upset" or "mad". Your wife (missus) will be angered accusing you of an indiscretion. The word "lippie" is a contraction of "lip stick" and finding this on your collar is being presumed as implicating you in an extra-marital affair. Under the foregoing circumstances you are unlikely to "get a leg over", that is to receive sexual favors from her.

*Had your wife simply been unwell - the other meaning of "crook"- she would be said of to have become or gone crook. Never "crook **at** you".*

181.A raw prawn is a:
    a. Smelly person
    b. Quack
    c. Rookie
    d. Road train

The correct answer is (b).

The reference to smell was made to confuse, as in a prawn is smelly and something "rank" stinks. This also is not a reference to rank amateur or rookie. Replies (a)and (c) are thus incorrect.

A "quack" is a charlatan. The latter term always meant an untrained person purporting to be a doctor but is now applied to any swindler. The term doctor is often shortened to "doc" and a duck quacks!

To "come the raw prawn" is to try and put one over someone or impose on somebody. The term may well have utility in dealing with a used car sales man; as in: "Don't come the raw prawn with me mate, this shit heap is not worth a cent over four grand!"

Lastly, whilst entirely inapplicable to this question, a road train is a large truck common to outback roads and not fit for a rookie to drive.

182.Rafferty's rules implies:
    a. A dingo's breakie
    b. A dog's breakfast
    c. Tidiness
    d. Rigid discipline

The correct answer is (b).

*Rafferty's rules means no rhyme or reason, hap-
hazard, without proper order but the author could not
find the origin of the expression. May be a Judge Rafferty
made rulings that did not follow any kind of order. Be that
as it may, a "dog's breakfast" is meant to be messy and is
the correct reply.*

*Dingo's breakfast - "breakie" being a diminutive for
breakfast – is nothing.*

**For question 183 – 188, consider the following
scenario:**

Berko, Stevo, Bruce, Timothy, and Chuck are at the
bar having a yarn over a couple of coldies. Bruce has
just claimed to have shagged a rather grouse bird.
Jonsey over hears the conversation. Answer the
following questions:

183.Pertaining to Bruce what is likely true:
    a. He will be a grumble-bum
    b. He will be like a pork chop in a synagogue
    c. He may be likened to a rat with a gold
       tooth
    d. It is his shout

The correct answer is (c).

*The vignette describes a bar scene. These boys are
all mates judging by the adoption of the informal first
names. Timothy, should be "Timo" if he was as close to
the boys as the others. Chances are they are not as
friendly with him. Bruce is making the claim that he has
had a sexual encounter with a superb ("grouse"),
outstanding, or otherwise hard to get woman ("bird")[30].*

---

[30] The term "bird" is inoffensive to all but the most ardent feminists.

*Jonsey, who must be a mate (again by the familiarity he
displays and the contracted name-in this case surname of
Jones), is a little distant and may not have been seen. He
is clearly not the part of the first group of mates and may
have arrived at a different time or had already been there.
He surreptitiously overhears the conversation.*

    *Bruce having allegedly achieved what he claims to
have achieved will have no excuse to be a "grumble
bum", meaning a grumpy kill-joy. He will also be popular
unlike a "pork chop in the synagogue". This phrase is not
poking fun at Judaism and is not by any stretch of
imagination anti-Semitic. It simply reflects on the fact that
a non-kosher article will be unpopular in the synagogue.
Let me apologize in advance, nevertheless, if it may upset
any of my many Jewish friends and countrymen.*

    *Bruce having gained notoriety is the man of the
moment and will not need to shout as the achievement
deserves a complimentary round of beers from others, if
for no other reason to loosen his tongue to elaborate
further.*

    *A "rat with a gold tooth" is proud and Bruce can
aptly be thought to deserve that adjective.*

    184.Which of the men is most likely a Seppo?
        a. Bruce
        b. Chuck
        c. Timothy
        d. Neither

The correct answer is (b).

    *"Seppo" is the diminutive form of "septic tank"
which is rhyming slang for "Yank" that is in turn a
contraction of "Yankee" to mean an American. A septic
tank is a sewerage receptacle and whilst not flattering to
Americans is not intended to be an affront. It is just a
rhyming slang.*

"Chuck" is what Americans shorten Charles to and is popular with them. It is entirely un-Australian. To us "chuck" is to throw away, toss, or vomit.

185. How would Jonsey *not* address the quorum?
   a. Bull-fuck!
   b. Fair-dinkum?
   c. You beaut....Bruce baby!
   d. You're a rellie, mate!

The correct answer is (d).

All but the last reply are exclamations - be it positive or negative - as I shall shortly elaborate. Knowing that "relies" are your relatives you can decipher the last reply as meaning: "You are a relative of mine!" This is clearly nonsensical in the present context.

Everybody knows "bull shit" as meaning non-sense, a lie or stupid gibberish. Presumably the reference is to the worthlessness of the droppings. "Bull-fuck" is just a magnification.

Something "beaut" is, on the other hand, very positive. It is like saying "grand!" However "you beaut!" is an exclamation reflexive onto the third person. Meaning Jonsey is congratulating Bruce. The "baby" suffix is not mucho and used more by the "snagy[31]" men than the real "blokie" kinds but means as an endearment with some adjective attributes.

"Fair dinkum" is the truth. You may use it to ask a question as in: "Fair dinkum?" or to seek clarification or to exclaim.

---

[31] Snag is an acronym for *Sensitive New Age Guy* but really is extrapolated to an effeminate man.

186. Which would *not* be an apt reply to Jonsey?
    a. Too true
    b. Aah, G'day you big poof
    c. Paper yabber
    d. Watta' ya' reckon?

The correct answer is (c).

A "paper yabber" is a letter and it would not be an apt reply to Jonsey's comment. To "yab" or "yabber" is to talk incessantly and a letter, being highly un-macho, is referred to thus. I am lead to believe the word takes its root from an aboriginal language.

"Too true" means to magnify but "watta' ya reckon" is a corruption of "What do you reckon?" meaning to pose the question in reverse. Essentially it asks: "Do you claim I am a liar?"

Reply (b) is based on the fact that Jonsey was not a part of the original gathering and may not have been seen up to when he identified himself by his comment. "Aah" is an excited exclamation, like "Oh, there you are!" "G'day" is the quintessential Australian greeting upon first seeing someone and not a salutation as an American Bank Teller might say: "Good Day Sir, Have a nice day!"

I scarcely need to go over "poofter" or its diminutive "poof" meaning a homosexual man save to explain that in this scenario it is an endearing comment and said without malice.

187. Based entirely on the names, who is likely to be the most aggressive of the men:
    a. Timothy
    b. Bruce
    c. Berko
    d. Jonsey

The correct answer is (c).

"Berko" literally means to have a fight and presumably this bloke got that nickname because of a reputation for scuffles.

188. What has Bruce actually achieved?
   a. He has shot an uncommon fowl
   b. He is not pissing in his mates pockets
   c. Bruce is all sorted with a good sort
   d. Bruce is likely to be as ugly as a box of blow-flies

The correct answer is (c).

In this context a "bird" is a woman not a "fowl" and shagging is sexual intercourse and is not a hunting sport – well!

To be "sorted" is to be "fixed up", "lined up", or simply "in business". A "good sort", on the other hand, is an attractive woman. Seeing that Bruce is all excited about his achievement and the boys are all complimentary, it is unlikely that he will be really ugly, that is "uglier than a box of blowflies" making reply (d) a poor one.

All indications support that these guys are all close mates, suggesting that Bruce is indeed "pissing in his mates pockets"- meaning he is quite chummy with the men. Witness the reference to proximity: If one who is that close to another was to relieve himself the stream is likely to land in the coat pocket of his chum!

189. You are in the dunny choking the brown dog, what would be in order?
   a. A pack of turd tickets
   b. A big spit
   c. Both (a) and (b)
   d. Neither (a) nor (b)

*The correct answer is (**a**).*

"Chocking the brown dog" is an obscene reference to defecation where faeces is likened to a brown dog and the anal sphincter the hands that may wring the neck of such a beast. "Poo" or "turd" tickets is a reference to "toilet tissues" making reply (a) correct.

A big spit is vomitus and is not related.

190. If you had to "use the Jerry 'cause the John is Cactus", what has just transpired?
    a. You had to rely on your intuition since the hired hand was unable to perform the requisite task
    b. Since your toilet was broken you were obligated to use a chamber-pot
    c. A hit man was hired to rid you of the problem that the authorities could not effectively address
    d. A threat was not effective and thus frank violence is called for.

*The correct answer is (**b**).*

The "jerry" is the "chamber-pot" and probably takes its root from "Jerry-can". The "John" is a "dunny" or toilet. Something is "cactus" when it is busted. Put it all together and you have the situation that is posed in reply (b).

191. Joe Bloggs had his Jocks down when a Joe Blake surprised him. What happened?
    a. Some bloke was having a shit when a snake slithered by
    b. Mr. Bloggs was having a root when his lover's husband presented
    c. A baby kangaroo has been surprised by a rattle snake
    d. The first title fighter was caught off guard by the second boxer

The correct answer is (a).

"Joe Bloggs" is a name given to any man whose name is unknown. It is like the "John Citizen" that is used as an example on the governmental application forms. "Joe Blake", on the other hand is a rhyming slang for snake. "Jocks" are male underwear and thus it transpires that our mystery man has his under wear down when a snake chances by. I won't elaborate any further.

A baby kangaroo is a "Joey" not a "Joe Bloggs". Also there are no rattle snakes in Australia!

192. An ocker is meeting a wog's oldies, he is most likely to say:
    a. G'day you old poof
    b. Sorry I rocked up in my jocks
    c. G'day, Aya gawoing?
    d. Nice knickers!

The correct answer is (c).

An "ocker" or "okker" is the genuine article. It is typically said as an "ocker Aussie" and means a non-migrant for more than a few generations, typically of Anglo-Saxon decent. The term is an affectionate one but there is almost a hint of "roughness" or "unpolished edges" about such a person. This may just be in the migrant circles though because the "ocker" invariably is unable to endear himself to older migrants where the clash of cultures may be too significant to easily circumnavigate. I am struggling to transmit the sentiment well but this fellow is a rather boorish man innocent of airs and graces, the archetypal "bull in the china-shop" if you will.

With the above descriptor in mind it is easier to study the replies in turn. The scenario is of a visit by this man to the household of a migrant (wog) to meet his/her parents (elders). One's elders are affectionately called "oldies" in much the same way that one's relatives are called "relies." Reply (a) is clearly false as no matter how uncouth this bloke may be he knows not to refer to elder-folk the way he may call his mate in the pub. "G'day you old poof" literary means: "Hello, You old homosexual man"!

To "rock up" is to front up or appear. As in: "Where the bloody hell have you been? You have rocked up two hours late!"

Our man is apologizing for appearing in his under wear! This is also clearly not likely, making reply (b) incorrect. Whilst we are at it let me explain that whereas "jocks" or men's shorts are unflattering to the male physique, knickers are items of feminine intimate apparel and are invariably exciting. Again I doubt our ocker is likely to comment on an old lady's intimate apparel nor is she likely to have presented herself thus.

The only correct reply is (c) meaning "Hello, how are you going?" which is a typical greeting neither too formal nor too casual.

193. A poddy dodger is playing possum, chances are:
    a. He was seen to have been negligent
    b. He has lost his marbles
    c. He is after favors
    d. A crocodile is involved

The correct answer is (a).

A "poddy-dogger" is a cattle thief, pure and simple. The term applies however to a station hand who is entrusted with the duty of tending the herds but he may make off with unbranded beasts when he can. Clearly a worse proposition in that a position of trust is abused. If he is "playing possum" he is "lying low" or is being scarce. The term is a reference to the possum being a timid little animal avoiding discovery. One's marbles are intellectual attributes of a person and the loss of marbles implies demented behavior. This means response (b) is not an apt response.

194. If you sit on a beer, you are likely to have:
    a. Questionable conduct
    b. Short arms and deep pockets
    c. Lots of mates
    d. Hemorrhoids

The correct answer is (b).

If you are drinking rather slowly, making a drink last longer than your mate's, you may be accused of "sitting on your beer". The implication is you are delaying ordering the next round of drinks (shouting your turn). Such a person, or indeed any one regarded as being too thrifty, is said to have "short arms and deep pockets"- a brilliant descriptor for not being able to reach the end of his pocket.

195.How are a thingamajig, thingemebob, and thingo
   different?
    a. They are all watchamecallits
    b. Thingo is the same as thingamabob but the
       opposite of thingamajig
    c. Both (a) and (b) are correct
    d. Two thingamajigs makes one thingo

The correct answer is (a).

These are all terms for when you can not recall the name of an item (only applies to inanimate objects). If you can not recall the name of a person, you say "whatshisface"!

196.If you look pretty swank, you are:
    a. A bit of a scrubber
    b. Scrubbing up alright
    c. Definitely a purse-carrying nancy boy
    d. You routinely swindle unsuspecting
       persons

The correct answer is (a).

Something that is "pretty swank" is attractive but the possessor knows it, as it were. This person is a scrubber. The implication is that he or she attends hard to grooming so as to be swank.

If you "scrub up alright" you are capable of looking presentable but are too macho to do this routinely. It is not the done thing to be seen too swanky on a cattle station for example but you may well scrub up to go to the next property and ask the Smith's girl out to tea.

A "nancy boy" is an effeminate man. If you are jealous of a swank you may accuse him of being a poof or a nancy boy. However, it is generally untrue. This means the adjective "definitely" renders the response (c) erroneous.

197."Stone the crows what blooming drover's dogs?!"
means:

    a. I am awe inspired by the sheep dog

    b. I am besotted by the elegance of the item
of lingerie

    c. An anguished displeasure at the inaptitude
of the dog

    d. A cry of joy at the number of attendees at
your function

The correct answer is (b).

"Stone the crows" is an exclamation of outer joy in the vast majority of cases. "Blooming" is an adjective for emphasis.

A drover's dog in the literal sense is a sheep dog that musters the beasts. It is very cleverly applied to a bra! It too rounds them up and holds them together!

198.You have invited Jacko to a party and tell your
mutual mate about it. His reply is: "Pigs bum! He
is a piker". Imagine this mate is fair dinkum and in
the know, then

    a. Jacko will probably get drunk in your party
the way he always does

    b. He will probably not come

    c. He has a reputation for late arrival

    d. The mate is joyous at the prospect of
seeing Jacko who has a reputation for
being the life of the party

The correct answer is (b).

The phrase "pig's bum" or "pig's arse" is an exclamation of distrust, skepticism, or disdain. It is like the British saying "Garbage! What a load of codswallop". The mate is accusing Jacko as being a "piker" or a wowser or kill-joy. Americans would call such a person a "party-pooper". In the present context Jacko is being accused of having promised to come to the party but at the last minute he will come up with some excuse not to go. That is; pikes out.

199. A lady muck is a:
   a. Woman with airs and graces but no substance
   b. Half empty glass of beer
   c. Glass of beer poured from the bottom half of the beer bottle
   d. Pack of lamingtons

The correct answer is (a).

200. Where does Dame Edna live?
   a. Mont Albert
   b. Marriot Lakes
   c. Moonie Ponds
   d. Mosman

The correct answer is (c).

Dame Edna Everage is the alter ego of Barry Humphries, a famous and talented comedian, responsible also for the lecherous Sir Les Paterson. Barry Humphries appearing in his drag costumes as Dame Edna has interviewed many a famous person. She has a flamboyant personality and wears outlandish gowns. In the 1970s the then Prime Minister of Australia, Gough Whitlam, awarded her the title of "Dame" of the British Empire. She is a housewife who lives in Moonie Ponds, Melbourne.

Glossary:

This glossary has not been intended to be exhaustive. It introduces, by and large, choice words to help you answer the questions in the test papers. There are comprehensive dictionaries available for the more discerning readers.

A

Ace Excellent. Extremely positive. Presumably a reference to the high value of this card in card games.

Aggro Someone who is aggravated or upset about something. By extension a short tempered person.

Alkie A contraction of "alcoholic".

Amber nectar Beer.

Ankle biter A toddler.

Ant's pants (Antz pants) To be proud of oneself. Being fashionable or specially talented. Someone who reckons he/she is FIGJAM. (Read on!)

Apple muncher A native of Tasmania. This being a slight on the fact that this state is famous for its apples (and potatoes) and is also known as the apple isle.

To be Apples! Everything is or will be okay.
("She is/will A beautiful or particularly pleasant woman.
be apples!")

Aerial ping Aussie Rules Football.
pong
Arse over tit To trip or fall over.

To get one's To get moving on a particular action.
Arse into gear

Arse about Something is back to front.
face
Arsed out Dismissed.

Avo Diminutive form of avocado.

Arvo Afternoon.

Aussie An Australian.

Ay? Also quite commonplace in New Zealand and
(Also said as: is used to confirm, emphasize or question
eh?) what was said.

AV Jennings Refers to one's first marriage.
AV Jennings is a builder in Australia
specializing in building inexpensive houses
for young married couples.

Awning over Refers to a man's beer belly; the toy shop
the being the male reproductive organs.
toy shop

Acres
(Achers)

Testicles.
A play on words with "acres" coming from "achers" being what would happen if someone kicked you in the testicles.

B

Back of
Beyond
(Black stump)

Also called back of **Burke** and is as far as one can get away from civilization.

Back hander

A bribe.
Also in its more literal sense may mean to strike someone.

Your **old Bag**
(Battle ax)

A highly offensive (to women) term to describe one's wife.

To **Bag**
someone

Defamatory remarks about someone. To obtain sexual favors from a girl. (*Vulgar*)

Bail out

To leave some premises.
Can also mean, in the strict sense, posting bail to free someone from the remand centre.

Bail up

A scuffle.

Banana
Bender

A Queenslander. It is a slight on the fact that they are said to have nothing better to do than to bend bananas. This state grows bananas commercially.

Bang on	Right at. Spot on. Like "I'll be there bang on seven!"
Banged up	To be pregnant. Up the duff.
To **bang like a dunny door** in a storm	A reference to a cheap harlot. Dunnies (outhouses) are typically hastily put together in wooden planks. In the present context the suggestion is that the woman in question makes loud noises during sexual intercourse.
A **Bar fly**	A man typically an older gentleman who has nothing better than to spend his entire day in the pub, literally from dusk to dawn.
Barbie	A barbecue(B.B.Q).
Have a **Barney**	A fistfight or scuffle.
Barrack	To support a team most often the Australian Rules Football code. Aussie rules is popular in Melbourne.
To **give something** a **Bash** or a **Burl**	Also known as "having a go", this is a half concocted attempt at a task one is ill-prepared or poorly schooled in the performance of.
Bathers	The term used to describe swimming costumes in Victoria .
Battler	A person making piss poor wages despite doing an honest day's work.

Beanie A must have bogan fashion accessory. A woolen cap.

You little Beauty! Bewdy! Bewdy mate! (You little ripper!) Excited approval.

Beer o'clock This is the "you beauty" time of the day when you down tools and head to the bar for a few beers.

To give someone a **Bell** Refers to the telephone.

Berko An aggressive gentleman. One taken to fits of rage however slightly provoked.

Better Half (or other half) Your spouse. A word implying a great deal of familiarity and refers to the half that completes you.

To have a **Bex and a lie down** Bex powder was a popular pain-reliever composed of aspirin, phenacetin, caffeine (or some say codeine). The housewife may have taken a Bex and had a lie down or may have recommended this to others for a whole host of ailments. Unfortunately the caffeine (or codeine) would cause an addiction that ultimately caused many cases of analgesic nephropathy and renal failure in the 1960s and

70s due to the cancer causing phenacetin.

Bikkies	An affectionate term to describe biscuits(cookies). It is also applied to money the same way that an American might refer to money as dough!
To **big note** oneself	Same as being a FIGJAM.
Billabong	A watering hole. A brook.
Billy (As in: "Billy tea")	Typically in relation to a kettle brought to boil over a campfire. A cup of tea made in the above manner.
Billy lids	A rhyming slang for "kids".
Bingle	A prang. An automobile accident.
To put the Bite on	To press someone for something that may even be yours in the first place and you are aiming to get back. Usually in relation to repayment of a loan.
Black Stump	Same as **Back of Beyond.**
"Something **even Blind Freddy could see!"**	Used if an obvious event, feature, or hint is grossly missed.
Bloke	A man.

Bloody oath....	This is a firm approval of something. Usually as exclamation.
Ugly as a **box of Blowflies**	Someone really ugly.
The Blower	Telephone.
Blowies	Blow flies.
To Bludge (Bludger)	A lazy person who whilst perfectly fit chooses to live off welfare hand outs is a bludger and the act is to bludge. Borrowing never intending to replace can also be called bludging.
True **Blue**	Something or someone who is the real Australian.
Having a Blue	A barney, a fight or an argument.
To have Bob as one's uncle	When all is well. Witness the statement: "If you study hard you will get a good earning job and then Bob is your uncle!"
Bogan	A popular term also known as a Westy (in Sydney) to describe essentially a ruffian.
To bolt	To make a hasty retreat.
Bonza (Bonzer)	An expression of delight.

Boomer	A Kangaroo.
Booze Bus	A police vehicle fitted out as a breath analysis station for apprehension of drunken drivers. Also a name given to the courtesy buses that certain clubs run to avoid their patrons having to drive under influence of alcohol.
You little **Bottler**	An expression of delight as with "you little beauty!" It means something has gone your way.
Your Blood is worth Bottling!	You would say this when someone has done you a good turn or has provided a service of immense import to you.
Brass	This is same as saying bikkies. You may say something like: "Do not blow all your brass on flowers, she is married!"
Brass razoo	Indicates a paucity of finances.
Brekky	A contraction of the word "breakfast".
Bricky's cleavage	A bricky is a brick layer. Given the heat they tend to wear shorts and not uncommonly the top of the buttocks can be exposed, particularly as they bend over.
To be choking the Brown dog	This is a euphemism for defecation.

Brumby	Wild horse.
Buckley's chance	None to a very slim chance at success. A forlorn hope. William Buckley was a convict transported to Australia who absconded from Port Phillip in 1803 and managed to survive in the bush when the aborigines confused him with a god given his large built and blonde hair and beard. He lived with them for 32 years ultimately to give himself up in 1835 and serve as a police tracker in Tasmania. Also another school of thought has it that Buckleys & Nunn was a store in Melbourne and "Nunn" rhymes with none.
Bugger	Legally means to perform an act of sodomy. It is typically taken to mean extreme fatigue as in "I am absolutely buggered." It may also be an expression of disappointment or excitement.
To do **Bugger all**	Doing absolutely nothing.
Bugger me dead!	Extremely shocked at something.
Bugger off!	An invitation for you to leave or reconsider your proposal! If asked as a question it can mean that you aren't believed or it may be an expression of surprise.
To go to Buggery	To truly ruin something.

To be **Built like a brick shit house**	Something or someone is of very strong construction.
Bull dust	Implies a lot of hot air. Much emphasis being placed on nothing.
Bum	An arse. One's bottom. Also used to describe a dero or down and outer.
Bundy	Bundaberg rum that is typically had as a mixed drink with coke, as in "Bundy and Coke".
To not be able to arrange **a piss up in a brewery!**	Incapable. Useless. A bloke incapable of performing the simplest of tasks.
Bung	To place upon. Such as: "Just bung your arse down and shut up mate!"
Bunyip	A mythical creature from aboriginal folklore said to frequent billabongs.
To give something a (good) **Burl**	To give something that you have not done before, a try. Typically an ill-prepared effort.
Bush-bash	Forcing one's way through untouched bush.
Bush pig	An unattractive woman.

Bush telegraph	Gossip.
To Bust one's Chops (Busted)	To get someone into trouble or more usually to get into trouble with the law, like a speeding ticket and the like.
BYO	An acronym for *B*ring *Y*our *O*wn. Many restaurants allow you to bring your own bottle of wine and charge you only for the corkage.

C

Cactus	Dead, destroyed, or de-commissioned.
Cakehole	Your mouth.
Captain Cook	Rhyming slang for having a "look".
To **Cark** it	To die. Deceased.
Chalkie	A teacher. The reference is to a blackboard and chalk.
Chew the fat	A quorum. Tantamount to a brain-storming session.
Chinwag	Having a good yarn. Spinning tall-tales.
Chip off the old block	An offspring that resembles his father in physical or other attributes.

Spitting Chips   Being very angry. I fancy the idea was that if you are angry you would bite a tree trunk in shear frustration and spit the chips.

Chippie   A carpenter.

To Choof off   To be on one's way. To depart as in: "I might as well choof off, there are no half decent Sheilas here!"

Chook   A chicken, rooster or hen.

May your Chooks turn into emus and kick your shithouse down   An emu is a flightless bird not much smaller than an ostrich. You may make this statement if you are not very happy with what someone has done to you. A half-hearted curse.

Chuck   To throw something. Very commonly applied to vomiting though.
You may chuck things that are not thrown usually, as in "I chucked a flamin' spaz attack" to mean I got really disenchanted with someone.

Chunder   To chuck your guts. A Vomit.

Clayton's   Claytons was cordial marketed under the catch cry: "A drink you have when you do not want to have a drink!" The implication being avoidance of alcohol. If something is Clayton's it is broken, dodgy, or of questionable integrity. A fake.

Cobber	A mate, a close friend.
A Cock up	A terrible error or omission. I believe the American military has an acronym FUBAR standing for *f*ucked *u*p *b*eyond *a*ll *r*epair. That is a cock up in Aussie.
Cock and bull story	A furphie. A tall tale put together with the express aim to defraud.
Cockroach	A resident of the state of New South Wales. New South Welshmen have a name for all other fellow Australians, witness Banana-bender (Queenslander) or Crow-eater (South Australian), and so forth. I have a mind to think that the term "cockroach" is to get back at them but equally well may pertain to the large number of cockroaches in Sydney.
Codswallop	Strictly British and means a lot of nonsense or a lie.
Codger	A grumpy old fellow. A crusty old bloke. One taken to telling stories when in the right mood but preferring to whinge about how undesirable modern times have become.
Coldie	A beer. A play on the chilled beverge.
Compo	A contraction of the phrase "Worker's Compensation". You are on compo if you got

hurt or claim to have been hurt at the work place. A favorite of blodgers.

Cop it sweet   To cop something is to take it without a question even if the hand you are dealt is far from just. You may "cop it on the chin" or "cop it sweet."

Cop shop   Police station.

Cozzie   Bathers or swimmers in New South Wales.

Crapper   The toilet. The reference is to where you may go to defecate, that is to have a crap. (*Vulgar*).

Crack onto   To make a pass at or try to chat up.

To **cream** something or someone   Generally refers to a team having been beaten by a huge margin but I repeatedly heard it at uni typically after a particularly good performance at an exam. "Mate! I creamed the second question."

Crikey!   An older phrase implying surprise. This had a resurgence thanks to the late Steve Irwin – The Crocodile Hunter.

Crook   A corrupt individual. As in: "Crook as a Queensland politician!" A sick person. As in: "Mate, I was crook as a dog Thursday avo." Less commonly being upset. "No mate, me old lady will go crook at me if I come to the pub again!"

All is **Crook in Muswellbrook**	Muswellbrook is a town in New South Wales. This phrase is again a rhyming slang implying one is having a bad lot in life. "Everything is gone to the dogs!"
Crow-eater	A resident of South Australia. The implication is that many crows are found in the outback South Australia.
Cruddy	Shonky. Hastily put together. Jerry built! The commodity is Clayton's.
Cunning as a shithouse rat	Very cunning and under handed.
A "**Cuppa**"	A contraction of "a cup of tea".
To be as **mad as a Cut snake**	Very angry indeed. The wriggling of the cut snake is likened to angry gestures!
To **cut the dog** in half	To fart.

D

Daks (Dacks)	A pair of trousers.

A **Dag** (something daggy)	In reality this is faeces attached to the wool on the rear end of a sheep. It is, however, used as a mildly critical or even an endearing remark to refer to someone. May be said thus: "Gee Steve you are such a dag to even ask her out." or "Don't be a dag, I am not gonna have you pay, it is my shout." In amongst the youth anything unfashionable, unattractive, or undesirable is daggy. "Dad! That is such a daggy jumper to wear."
Damp squib	An idiot. A squib being a small firecracker and a damp one not going off.
Damper	Bread bun cooked by the camp fire.
Dead cert	Absolute certainty.
Dead horse	Rhyming slang for tomato sauce (ketchup).
Dunny	An outhouse specifically, though now applied to any toilet by extrapolation.
Didgeridoo	An aboriginal wind musical instrument made of hollowed tree branches.
Digger	An older Australian soldier (specifically WW I veteran) and probably a reference to digging of trenches.
Dilly-bag	A carry-bag. A swag.

Dinki-di	As with true-blue, means something uniquely Australian.
To pay Dirt (on someone)	The younger Aussies use it to mean "mud-sling" or "name-call" but the term *actually* means to achieve success and reach the object of one's search. It is probably a mining term to mean your patch of dirt has produced good dividends.
Dodgy	Something suspicious or an item that is Clayton's.
Dog and bone	More rhyming slang. This one means the "telephone".
To cut the dog in half	Farting. I have no idea where this one has come from.
Dog's Breakfast	Very messy. Also said to be messier than inside a whore-house.
Dingo's breakfast	Nothing. A dingo gets up and gets going!
A Done Deal	A sure thing.
Done over	To be second best in a contest. Damaged or tainted.
Donger	*Vulgar*: Penis.

Donkey's years	An inordinately long time.
Drinking with the flies	To drink alone, that is the flies are keeping you company.
Drongo	A character, an idiot, someone who acts foolishly. May be an insult: "Who let that flamin' drongo in here!" or a joke: "You are a real drongo, mate!"
To drop one's bundle	A pregnant woman post-partum. To lose one's cool. To be rattled by the situation.
Dropping one's guts	Farting.
Drover's Dog	A bra. The same way that the sheep dog musters the animals, the bra also rounds up(the breasts) and holds them together!
Dry as a dead dingo's donger	*Vulgar*: Very dry indeed. The land is parched. Donger being a penis.
Up the Duff	Pregnant.
Duffer (To sink a Duffer)	An unproductive mine. If you sink a duffer you are going to bottom out. The expression actually refers nowadays to a piss-up session - This being a more modern expression meaning the same thing. As in: "Come on, Let's go sink a few duffers!" That is: "Lets

have a few drinks." Perhaps an empty beer glass is likened to an unproductive mine.

Dumper Pertaining to the sport of surfing, a wave that breaks suddenly hurling the rider down.

A Dunny door in a storm Something or someone making a loud noise. Refers also to a cheap harlot as a reference to noises made during intercourse. A woman of questionable morality.

Dunny budgie A fly.

Durry A cigarette, especially "roll-your-owns" and may mean more aptly a cigarette butt, or half smoked cigarette. There is a suggestion that this relates to a maker of tobacco, *Bull Durham*.

Dutch oven A game where you would pull the bed spread over your mates head and fart underneath. A favorite of teenagers!

E

Ear bashing A telling-off or constant badgering.

To eat a horse, and chase the jockey Being extremely hungry.

Esky	An insulated cool box to keep your beer cold. Coleman of Kansas makes a similar contraption.

F

Fags	Cigarettes. Younger Aussies will understand the Americanism, fag, that is a contraction of "faggot" to mean a homosexual man.
Fair crack of the whip!	A fair go. When said in protest it is intended for seeking justice, as in: "Fair crack mate, I paid for the last two rounds of beer, it is now your turn!" The simple cracking of the stockman's whip ought to have the cattle rounded up. To physically strike them with it is likened to an "unfair crack of the whip!"
Fair-go Mate!	Protesting the unfair hand you are being dealt.
Fair dinkum	someone or something really genuine.
Crack a Fat	*Vulgar*: An erection.
To **fart-arse** around	To dilly-dally. Horsing around.
Fat chance	A slim chance. Same as Buckley's chance.
"Flaming"	An adjective to describe a person, event, or commodity that is either specially satisfactory or particularly bad. Like: "That flamin'

bastard Joe damaged the car." Alternatively "I had a flaming good time at your party, mate!"

Flash as a rat with a gold tooth   Someone who has groomed oneself well. To be particularly proud of one's looks.

Flat chat   To be busy or going very fast. Applies often to work or driving.

To give something the Flick   To toss something out or leave someone.

Floater   Meat pie in thick pea soup or gravy.

Flog   This can be used to mean stealing, borrowing (usually not intending to replace), or selling (commonly of sub-standard goods). Witness: "Jacko is still trying to flog off them dodgy fridges." In this example the person is trying to sell shonky refrigerators. "Can I flog a smoke off you mate?" You are asking for a cigarette but clearly not going to replace it.

Footbrawl   A euphemism for football reflecting upon the more than occasional violence.

Footy   A contraction of the word "football" used regardless of the code. It does not apply to soccer, despite elsewhere this being the *real* football.

Fossicking   Prospecting for opals (usually). Loosely used to imply sniffing around for good deals or information.

Full as a boot Drunk.

Funny as a Something that is not funny. (*Sarcasm*)
fart in an
elevator

Funny farm A mental institution.

G

G'day A contraction of the salutation: "Good Day", as in have a good day but said as a greeting. Never used to bid someone farewell.

Galah Typically used along with an adjective; like "bloody galah", to refer to a person of little intellect or one who likes to jest. The term is a reference to the loud native bird of the parrot family.

To be Game To be brave at the face of adversity(or stupid for that matter).

To have a To have a look or "squeeze."
Gander

Garbo A contraction of the word "garbage collector."

Gasbag A chatterbox or someone who talks incessantly.

A Goer If an event is a goer it will definitely occur. A dead cert.

Going like hot cakes Used when something is very popular or being sold or otherwise given away rapidly.

To have gone to the dogs Typically refers to a place or some goods or services that were once optimal but have since severely dilapidated.

Good as Gold! A phrase used to imply a state of good repair. Imagine you have just been involved in a car accident and you get out investigating the damage. You are pleasantly surprised that there are no damages. As you get back in your wife says: "Any damages?" Your reply may well be "No, she is as good as gold!"

Goodo Okay! Very well.

Good oil Useful or first grade information.

Good on you! An expression of joyful satisfaction with an outcome or performance. Witness the scenario when your mate tells you he has just quitted a low paying unsatisfactory job and immediately landed a better post. Your reply may well be "Good on ya mate!"

To be as full as a Goog A goog is an egg. It is perceived to have little free space and an inebriated person may well be as full as a goog.

Come off it! A sarcastic reply to a rather far fetched statement. It is used to ridicule the purveyor of the furphy.

To be green around the Gills A rank amateur. An upstart.

Grazier A cattle farmer or owner of grazing land.

Grog A term for an alcoholic beverage but by default applies to beer.

Grouse Terrific.

Grumble-bum A person who habitually complains.

Grunter A harlot. A prostitute. (*Vulgar*)
The reference is to noise during sexual intercourse.

Gumsucker A native of the state of Victoria. The reference is to gum-trees (eucalyptus) and their alleged abundance in this state. They are also known as "Mexicans" given they live to the south of the river (Murray).

To be down the Gurgler The reference is to flushing or having water "gurgle" down the sink-hole. It implies an event having a bad outcome. An example may be: "Since Janet left my life is down the gurgler!"

| On a good wicket | A cricketing term which in common daily usage means to be on a good thing. Can also imply good luck by extrapolation. |

H

| Happy as a pig in a pool of shit | Very content. |

| Hard case | A close-minded person, resistant to change. A tough guy. |

| Hit the Frog and Toad | A rhyming slang for "hit the road". It means to leave, as in "I best hit the frog and toad before me missus knows I have been gone." |

| "Hoo-roo" | Bush salutation given with a brief wave typically from afar as you depart. This has had a revival thanks to Don Burke of the TV Show, "Burks Backyard"! |

| "Howzat?" | A contraction of "How is that?" Used to ask how something is. Typically said in self satisfaction in a rhetorical manner. Imagine someone challenges you to a task they deem you are not capable of performing upon the satisfactory completion of such a task you may well ask: "How is that?" |

I

Idiot box   The television.

Iffy   Pertains to "if" and implies suspect
                   undertakings. Circumspect.

J

**To be
"Jacked"
with
something**   To be most irritated and displeased or fed up
                   with something. In full it is being "jacked off"
                   and is a *vulgarism* with overtones of
                   masturbation.

**Jack-in-the-
box**   Someone who can not sit still.

Jackaroo   A male drover or a station hand, a cow boy.

Jillaroo   A cow-girl, a female drover.

Jerry   A chamber-pot to relieve oneself in the
                   middle of the night.

Jerry-built   Anything hastily put together and of inferior
                   construction.

A Jiffy   A little while. It is the same as a "mo"
                   (contraction of a minute), a "tick" (refers to
                   the clock ticking), or a "shake of the lamb's
                   tail"
                   Presumably this takes very little time.

To job someone	Same as a bifo, a fist-fight.
Jocks	Underpants (male). Never intended to be flattering to the male physique.
Joe Blake	Again rhyming slang this time to mean "a snake".
Joe Bloggs	A man, any man. It is like saying "some bloke" or "John Citizen".
Joey	A baby boomer. A young kangaroo before leaving the pouch.
The John	Not strictly Australian nor in favor but means the same as a dunny: An outhouse, or a toilet.
Journo	Journalist.
Jumper	A sweater.
Jumbuck	Sheep. This is a long shot but the term may be a corruption of "jump up"!

K

Kafuffle	A whole lot of fuss, a fight, an argument or other public disturbance or loud discourse.
Keen as mustard	Keen is a maker of mustard and condiments. The reference is to the "sharp bite" of the

mustard and refers to a person enthusiastic about some endeavor.

Kindy   A contraction of the German word "kindergarten".

King hit   A "right royal" blow during a scuffle. A definite or decisive punch and generally carries claims of unfairness or surprise. Ah, if I had a dollar for every time a guy with a broken jaw came to the practice and made the claim: " The bastard came from no where Doc and just King-hit me!"

Kip   The small flat piece of wood on which the two coins in "two-up" are placed. Also means a nap.

One's Kit   One's gear or clothes. As in: "I cracked a fat before she could get her kit off!" *Vulgar:* to mean that "I had an erection before she could get naked."

Kiwi   A New Zealander. This is a reference to the flightless bird, the Kiwi, native to that nation.

Knackered   Tired, exhausted (to the extreme).

Knickers   The female underwear.

Knock-off   A counterfeit product.

Knock shop	A brothel. The implication being that this is were you go to knock somebody up!
To Knock something	To criticize negatively.
Knocked back	Rejected.
Knocked up	Commonly means pregnant but loosely applied to just having sex.
Knock off time	Same as "beer o'clock" and means time to stop work and head to the pub.
"Whad-aya-know?"	"What do you know?" A phrase used in a familiar way to encourage conversation, really an invitation to gossip. It can be substituted for a friendly greeting.

L

Lady muck	A woman with pretentious airs and graces but with no substance.
Lame-brained	A buffoon.
Laughing gear	The mouth.
Lashing out	Specifically to get angry but applied also to doing something in excess.

Lav **(Lavvy)**	A diminutive form of "lavatory" and means an outdoor toilet.
To lead one up the **garden** path	An attempt at deception or to defraud a gullible person.
To take a **Leak**	Refers to urination. (*Vulgar*)
To get a leg over	*Vulgar*: To have sexual intercourse.
Lemon	An item that is Clayton's or inferior. Most commonly applied to an inferior automobile. Describes also a lesbian (homosexual female). (*Vulgar*)
"The lights are on but there is no one home"	To be a few snags shy of a barbie. Not too bright. Implies a dim person, a lame brain.
Lippie	A contraction of the word "lipstick".
Liquid amber	Beer.
Lollies	Sweets.
Lollywater	A diluted drink. An insult on the drink served by someone who is skimping on you.
A month of Sundays	An expression used for an outcome not being very likely as in: "Not in a month of Sundays will I squeal on my mates."

This is not unique to Australian English but nevertheless quite popular.

A long drink of water	A tall person.
Long neck or "longie"	A beer bottle that is not a stubbie.

M

To be as Mad as a cut snake	To be really angry. "Mad" in this context refers to anger not lunacy!
As Mad as a hater	The old milners used to soak hat rims in mercury to stiffen them and the mercury, being a neurotoxin, used to make them crazy. The reference therefore is to being quite mad.
Mapa-Tassie	Map of Tassie(Tasmania). Female pubic hair. A woman's bush (*vulgar*). Refers to map of the state of Tasmania, which is roughly triangular in shape.
Mate	A friend. An habitual companion.
Matilda	A bed roll for camping out. A sleeping bag.
Milk bar	The corner grocery store.

Missus	One's wife.
Mozzie	A mosquito.
Mollydooker	A left handed individual. No one seems to be able to explain this one to me but an old war veteran reckoned it was Irish in origin, putatively due to the currency of the name "Molly" there. I remain puzzled.
Moosh	The mouth.
More of (an entity) **than one can Poke a stick at**	A lot of something.
Middy	A measure of beer equivalent to 10 oz in NSW and 7 oz in WA.
Things are crook in Muswellbrook	Times are bad. Crook is a bad outcome in the present context.
Plates of Meat	Yet again more rhyming slang to mean one's "feet".
Mystery bag	A sausage. The implication is one never knows what the butcher has put into his sausages.

N

Nana   One's grandmother.

Nanna   A contraction of the word "banana".

Nappy   What the Americans call a diaper.

Narkie   A short tempered person. You are narkie if you are narked off at the slightest provocation.

Naughty   Sexual intercourse.

NCR Rating Acronym for *n*umber of *c*ans *r*equired before one may bed an otherwise unattractive girl (sobriety and the light of the day not withstanding).

Neddie or Neddy A horse. Originated from children's term for a beast of burden. Applies specifically to a race horse.

The Never Never Outback away from any civilization.

Nick off Piss off. An invitation to make oneself scarce.

Get Nicked! An invitation to nick off.

No-hoper Someone who is hopeless. One who is worst than tits on a bull. Of no practical benefit.

To be **"on the Nose"** To emit an unbecoming smell.

Nudey	Naked. Nude.

O

Ocker or Okker	Truly Aussie. The genuine article.
Off the Beaten Track	On a road not oft frequented.
"Off like a ..." [bride's nightie] **or** [Jew-boy's foreskin] **or** [prawns in the midday sun]	To beat a hasty retreat or abandon your location. A rapidly executed action. *Note*: A "nightie" is a night gown.
Oldies	Parents, elder-folk.
Once over	To check something out. Appraisal.
"On ya mate"	Contraction of "Good on you mate!"
Outback	The bush. The remote part of the nation.
To have a **bun in the Oven**	To be pregnant.

P

Pack of Poo tickets   A roll of toilet paper.

Paper yabber   To chatter is to yabber. A paper yabber is a letter.

To be all **paly-paly**   To be friendly with someone. Refers to pal.

To pash   Necking or foreplay. Reflects on the word "passion".

Pearler   Real good. Grouse. Excellent.

Perve *(noun)*
To Perve
(verb)   A contraction of pervert and means a lecherous man.
However, to "perve" is to eye someone lustfully.

Ps or P plates   A plate worn by "provisional drivers" which tell other motorists the driver is a new road-user. If you lose your licence for a serious offence you will have to go back to wearing this plate on your car.

Pie floater   A meat pie in pea soup.

Pigs bum or pig's arse   A phrase used to imply your disquiet about an incredulous assertion. As in: "Pig's bum! He was not crook. I saw him at the club drinking."

Piker

A kill-joy, a wowser, a person who may promise to perform a task then leave you "high and dry" typically at the last moment.

Pinch

To remove or borrow with or without permission irrespective of whether one intends to make restitution for the "pinching"!

To piss in someone's pocket

To ingratiate oneself to someone, to be on very familiar terms with a person. "All paly-paly!" Implies extreme proximity.

Pissed

Inebriated. Unlike the USA "pissed" _never_ means angry in this country only drunk.

Pissed off

Angry.

Plate of meat

Rhyming slang for "feet".

To play Possum

Trying to protect oneself from being discovered for an adverse act or an omission. Lying low.

Poddy-dodger

A station hand who makes off with unbranded cattle. A cattle thief.

Pommy or Pom

Appropriately presented this is an acronym "POHM" standing for *p*risoner *o*f *H*er *M*ajesty. This is a reference to an English person and is based on the fact that convicts were transported to the colonies such as Australia by the English.

Ponce	Originally was applied to a man who lives off the proceeds of having prostituted his wife. It now implies an effeminate man.
Driving the **Porcelain Bus**	Vomiting. The act of leaning over the toilet clutching the rim is likened to driving the Porcelain bus!
To feel as welcome as a **Pork chop** in a Synagogue	Unfit, disheveled, unwelcome. Out of sorts with oneself.
Pork Chop	A person given to fits of anger.
To score (get) one between the posts	*Vulgar*: The reference is to sexual penetration during intercourse and is borrowed from the football term for scoring a goal.
Postie	A contraction of the word "Postman".
Pot	A measure of beer. In Victoria and Queensland it will buy 10 Oz and was never formally regulated in Western Australia.
Prang	A car collision. An automobile accident or any other manner of accidental destruction. Like: "Don't prang the bloody rose bush as you take the flamin' laundry down!" Also a bingle.
Prawn	Shrimp.

The Raw Prawn	A gullible or unintelligent person. An uninitiated person.
Prezzy	A contraction of "present". Gifts or offerings.
To be as proud as a rat with a gold tooth	To be impressed with one's own appearance or achievements.
Pub	A bar.
To pull one's head in	Probably refers to a turtle and implies minding one's own business.
To pull up one's socks	To try and get an otherwise messy life into order.
Push-bike or **Pushy**	"Pushy" being a diminutive for the word and meaning a bicycle.

Q

Quack	A doctor with a bad reputation. I am given to believe that this is a reference to "doctor" sometimes being shortened to "doc" and a duck making a "quack" noise!
Quid	(*Archaic*) Not in current usage but meant Pounds in the old currency. Presently the term

is understood in the broader sense of ***money*** if one was to use it.

Not the full Quid	To be a snag short of a barbie. Not so bright. Unintelligent. A dim person.
To not be dead for Quids	Very well. Quite fit. Meaning that one would not die even if offered money!

R

Racing off	Hastily departing.
Rack off	An invitation to make one scarce. To get lost.
Rafferty's Rules	A right royal mess. Done without any rhyme or reason. A dog's breakfast.
The Rag	*Vulgar*: A harlot. Reference to a sanitary napkin.
Rat-bag	A sly dog! A charlatan. A man of poor moral standards.
Raw prawn	To impose on someone, to try and pull the wool over one's eyes.
Rellie	A contraction of the word "relative". A family member.
Righto!	Okay or that is right. Can also be written as "right on".

Ring-in   An imposter.

Rip off   To cheat. To copy, typically, an inferior version of a well sought after article. To swindle.

A Ripper   Grouse. Something really great.

Root   *Vulgar*: Sexual intercourse.

Rooted   *Vulgar*: Refers to above but means very tired.

Retched   Said as "rat shit" by the un-schooled and indicates extreme tiredness.

S

Australian Salute   Australia has a fly problem! Waving one's hands around to swat the flies is likened to a salute.

Salvo   A contraction of the ***Salvation Army*** which is a world-wide charitable organization.

To be sacked   To have been fired from work. Probably a reference to the act of being handed one's sack in which the employee might keep his belongings or tools of trade.

Sand-groper	A native of Western Australia. A reference to the great sandy expanses of this state.
Sangers (Sangas)	Sandwiches.
To be a **Snag short of a barbie**	Literally means to be a sausage short of a barbecue. Refers to being dim-witted.
Scallops	What Queenslanders call potato cakes which are fried patties of mashed potatoes.
Schooner	A measure of beer worth 15 oz in New South Wales and 9 oz in South Australia. Other states either do not use this measure or their measures are not standardized formally.
Scrounge around	To be sniffing around (usually looking for bargains). An unflattering term.
To Scrub-up well	A term - generally used endearingly - to describe a person who may have spent a good deal of effort to have him/herself appear neat and attractive. To be done up, or "all dolled up" as an American might say.
Septic Tank	An American. This is rhyming slang for "Yank" which in turn is a contraction of the word "Yankee".
Seppo	Now this one really separates men from boys! Seppo is a diminutive form of the word "septic tank" which is rhyming slang for "Yank" which in its own turn is a contraction of "Yankee" and means an American.

Servo	A contraction of the term "service station", where one refuels one's car.
Shag	Strictly British and means sexual intercourse.
Shank's pony	A pedestrian.
Shark bait (cake, biscuits, etc.)	A surfer. The reference is to shark attacks on the surfers.
Sheila	A woman. This term is in use but not in favor. It is not derogatory and should not upset anyone but the most rabid feminists.
She will be right!	Everything will be alright.
Shirty	Upset or angry. Probably a reference to the pulling and tugging men have at each others shirts before a fist-fight ensues.
Shonky	Unreliable, circumspect goods, suboptimal merchandise. Clayton's version.
To Shoot through	Hasty departure.
Having someone by the **Short and curlies**	*Vulgar*: This is a reference to pubic hair and implies having relinquished control of the circumstances in a manner that greatly compromises one.

To have Short arms and deep pockets	Stingy, overtly thrifty.
Shout	To treat someone to something. By far and away applies to purchasing rounds of beer.
To not Shout even in a shark attack	This is a very clever play on the word "shout" the implication is being tight-fisted and disinclined to buy your round of beers.
Shove off!	An invitation to depart. Need not be aggressive such as: "Lets shove off at around five this arvo to get to Liverpool on time."
Sickie	A contraction of "sick leave" and refers to claiming of sickness benefits by fraudulent means. Put another way this is the tradition of "chucking a sickie" to go to the beach.
To Sit on a beer	Taking long to drink a beer, so as to delay shouting the next round!
A Slash	*Vulgar:* Used in masculine circles to mean urination.
A Slab of grog	A presentation pack of beers containing 24 cans.
More slippery than a well-Vaselined eel	A sly or sleazy man. A superb use of imagery, witness how difficult it may be to hang on to a well vaselined eel!
Slog	Hard work, hard yakka.

Sloppy joe	A loosely fitting(over-sized) sweater
Smoko	The word itself is a contraction of "smoke" and means a tobacco break or a coffee break.
Snag	A sausage.
Snake	A person of sub-total scruples. A charlatan.
A Sook!	A very sensitive person who is readily annoyed or disheveled. A cry-baby. The term is said to take origin from Yorkshire, England where an un-waned calf would be a "suck" pronounced with Yorkshireman's accent as "sook." The sook in our context is such "a baby" as to not yet be waned off milk!
I will Sort it!	A statement used to make conciliatory gestures when something is not quite right, whether one means to rectify the error or not. The reply may be apt to the following angry utterance: "Your bloody dog pissed all over my pansies!"
To call a Spade a Spade	An honest and unblemished representation of the truth. However typically it implies that sensitivity and tact is not exercised in such a representation.
To call a Spade a Shovel	A clever play on words to imply the opposite of the above. The event is retold in a tainted manner. A dishonest or fanciful representation. Clearly a reference is being made to digging

in both scenarios but the intricacies of the phrase escapes the author (and I am calling the spade, a spade!)

Sparky (Sparkie)	An electrician.
The big Spit	Vomitus.
To Spit the dummy	The dummy is an infant's pacifier. The term implies anger over what may be otherwise trivial. That is, an infantile reaction is being alleged. However in daily usage, the term by extrapolation is applied to any angry reaction.
A good **Sport**	Someone who is good about either losing or winning. In the former instance taking the loss in his stride and in the latter not likely to gloat.
A good **Sort**	A pretty *woman.* (The term is gender specific.)
To be **Sprung**	Caught in a compromised position.
Spunk (Spunky)	An attractive person. Unlike "good sort" this term is not gender specific.
A Squatter	A usurper of someone else's property.
To have a **Squeez**	To look at something.

A Stick in the mud	A boresome individual. A wowser, or someone who is no fun to be around.
Sticky-beak	A gossip or nosey person.
Stone the crows!	An utterance of shock at something.
Streuth! (Strewth!)	An exclamation being a corruption of "It is the truth!"
Strine	"Australian" in the sense of the spoken language. Transcribed as may be pronounced in accent.
To be Stroppy	To be in a bad mood or cross with someone.
Stubby	A local bottle of beer as opposed to the long-necked bottle.
To not give a Stuff	*Vulgar*: To not care about something, an event, or someone. Witness the statement: "I do not give a stuff if her father owns a brewery, she is one ugly bird!" Meaning that the man does not care for the girl despite any advantages knowing her may offer. "The owning of brewery" is not to be taken literally, it is to imply incentive!
Stuffed	*Vulgar*: Very tired "Stuff" is to imply sexual penetration.

To pull up **Stumps**	A cricketing term pertaining to the end of the match when the stumps are removed and is used to mean leaving.
Surfie	A contraction of "surfer".
Swag	A bag or back-pack in which the swagman (wanderer)'s belongings are placed.
To look pretty **Swank** **(swankie)**	Well-groomed or of unusually impeccable dress-sense. Often used unflatteringly or in jealous overtones.
Siphoning the Python	*Vulgar:* Used in masculine circles to mean urination.
No Sweat!	"No worries"

T

Ta	Thanks. A diminutive.
Tat or tad	A little of something. A small quantity.
Taswegian	A Tasmanian.
Tea	The evening meal.

Tee up   The term is borrowed from golf and implies preparation for an event. As in: " No worries mate, I will tee up a meeting with the boss."

Bush Telly   Looking up at the stars, at a camp-fire, or somewhere into the distance. The implication being one of nothing better to do.

Thinga-me-jig   Substituted when one can not recall name of an object to which is being referred. As in "Give me that [*inability to recall*]thinga-me-jig."

Thing-eme-bob   A thinga-me-jig!

Thingo   Another form of thinga-me-jig. Again means that thing which one can not recall.

Thongs   You want to see women in thongs in USA not in Australia! Sadly as opposed to the American thongs that are scandalously brief under-garments, our thongs are rubber sandals. A must for the summer wardrobe of all discerning bogans.

"Thugby"   A derogatory term implying Rugby being played by thugs. There is a famous saying: "Soccer is a game for thugs played by gentlemen and Rugby is a game for gentlemen played by thugs."

A Tick   A short time. A moment. Presumably this is a reference to the ticking of the clock.

To have Tickets on Oneself	Antz pants. To be so full of oneself as to have printed tickets to the show!
The tide has gone out	There is no more beer in the glass.
Tight-arse	A frugal person, a miser, too thrifty.
Tinnie	A tin in Australia is a can in USA, and a tinnie is an affectionate reference to a beer tin!
To crack a Tinnie	To open a can of cold beer.
Couple of Tinnies short of a slab	Dim-witted. Same as: "A couple of snags shy of a Barbie!"
Too right!	An enthusiastic affirmation.
Tomahawk	This is a battle-ax of the American (red) Indians but in Australia refers to a rough-shearer of sheep. A station hand that repeatedly nicks the beast's skin as if shearing with a tomahawk.
To take a Trick	Typically used in the negative as: "Poor Joe just can't take a trick!" and means a person is constantly unlucky.
True Blue	Really Australian. An okker Aussie. The fair dinkum article.

Tucker	Food.
Tucker-bag (Tucker-box)	Lunch bag or box.
Going Twenty to the dozen	Going very quickly. A hasty retreat. Also something you may be wanting to give away. In the latter sense implying plentifulness.
Two-up	A "head-or-tails" game popularized by the ANZAC (*A*ustralian and *N*ew *Z*ealand *A*rmy *C*orps) soldiers. This is a game where two coins are tossed into the air and bets are taken on how they may land.

U

Uee	A "U" turn. Although in this country you do not make a "U" turn, you "chuck a uee!"
Underdaks or undies	Underpants. By and large applied to the male undergarment and as such unflattering. (*Gender Specific*)
Uni	A contraction of the word "University".
Up a gum-tree	To be in a spot of bother. In a quandary.
To be Up oneself	Self-congratulating.

Ute	A utility van, a light commercial vehicle.

V

Veggies	A contraction of the word "vegetables".
Vegemite	A breakfast spread very high in Vitamin B12.

W

To Wag school	To skip school, truancy.
Walkabout	Traditional aboriginal period of soul-searching and seeking of enlightenment when the individual would have isolated himself from the community. In our context the word means being absent or having departed. Can also be used for loss of an inanimate object; thus: "Mom! The scissors have gone walk-about again!"
Walkover	An easy task. "A walk in the park."
Wallop	To strike or hit with a massive blow.
A Walloper	A Police officer. A constable.
A Wally	A careless or unintelligent person. This older term was re-popularized by the Water Authority's water restriction campaign with

the slogan: "Don't be a Wally with water!"

Backroom Waltz	"Discipline" dished out at the Police Station, illegally.
Wanker	*Vulgar*: Literally one who masturbates but applied to a fool or dim person.
To come out in the **Wash!**	As in "something ironing itself out!" Meaning self-rectification of an adverse set of circumstances.
The Watering hole	The hotel or pub.
Wedding tackle	*Vulgar*: Penis.
A Wharfie	A longshoreman or a dockworker.
To give something **a Whirl**	To have a go at something without possession of all the requisite skills.
Wongi	(*Archaic*): A friendly yarn. This is a story that is not intended to be a malicious rumor.
Wossat?!	A contraction of "What is that?" Used in exclamation when you did not catch what was said.
To be on a **good Wicket**	Cricketing term to imply being on to a good thing.

Willy	A penis.
To put the Wind up someone	To frighten someone. To seek to intimidate.
Whinge	To complain incessantly.
Witchetty grubs	These are the larvae of moths and beetles and are considered something of a delicacy by the aboriginal Australians. The Grubs may be up to 15cm long and are eaten raw or cooked. They are said to taste like scrambled eggs. As the grubs' bore-hole leaves wood scraps tantamount to saw-dust at the base of the plant they populate, they are easy to identify and harvest.
To chuck a Wobbly	To throw a tantrum.
Wog	The term initially was an acronym for a "*w*esternized *o*riental *g*entleman" and did not have racist connotations. Later it became a slang term for a person of Mediterranean extraction and took on a deragtory innuendo. It is wrongly applied to anyone who is not of Anglo-Saxon heritage and has become more politically acceptable than it was a decade ago. In a perverse way it has even become fashionable to be a wog.
Wonky	Unstable or unsteady.
Wood & water Joey	A (typically young) station hand put to menial tasks. A joey is an immature Kangaroo still in

the pouch. This implies youthfulness of the young station-hand. Fetching of wood and water is indicative of unskilled labor.

Woop Woop   A long way from civilization. Back of Burke.

Wowser   A killjoy or prude.

Write off   A total disaster. Most commonly applied to an automobile "written-off" by the insurance broker as beyond reasonable means for salvage.

Y

Yabber, Yab,   To chatter or speak incessantly.

Yabbie   Freshwater crayfish.

Yakka   Work. Usually physically demanding.
(Hard Yakka)

Yank   A contraction of "Yankee" meaning an American.

A Yarn   A tall tale. Generally a fabricated version of what actually happened!

Yobbo   A dero. A down-and-outer. A slob.

Z

To catch some To go off to sleep.
Zees

Zebra Pedestrian crossing.
crossing

Zonked Truly exhausted. Very tiered indeed.

Appendix:

Banjo Paterson's Waltzing Matilda[32]

Oh! there once was a *swagman* camped in a *Billabong*,
Under the shade of a *Coolabah tree*;
And he sang as he looked at his old *billy boiling*,
"Who'll come a-*waltzing Matilda* with me?"
Who'll come a-*waltzing Matilda*, my darling?
Who'll come a-*waltzing Matilda* with me?
Waltzing Matilda and leading a water-bag --
Who'll come a-*waltzing Matilda* with me?
Down came a *jumbuck* to drink at the water-hole,
Up jumped the *swagman* and grabbed him with glee;
And he sang as he stowed him away in his *tucker-bag*,
"You'll come a-*waltzing Matilda* with me."
Down came the *Squatter* a-riding his thoroughbred;
Down came Policemen -- one, two and three.
"Whose is the *jumbuck* you've got in the *tucker-bag*?
You'll come a-*waltzing Matilda* with me!"
But the *swagman* he up and he jumped in the water-hole,
Drowning himself by the *Coolabah tree*;
And his ghost may be heard as it sings in the *Billabong*
"Who'll come a-*waltzing Matilda* with me?"

---

[32] The poem appears in its entirety given its immense importance to our nation. The words and phrases used through out the book are italicised to illustrate this point.

References:

I have cross-referred to the following publications but regularly drew blanks from them. It appears as though many of the colloquialisms remain shrouded in mystery. They all had "wog" and "digger" and the other more common terms but sadly, with the exception of the ABC radio series-word of the day, there were no real in-dept analyses.

My best source has proven to be the word of mouth that my older patients either willingly gave or had "extracted" and it is to them that I owe a great debt of gratitude.

1. Wilkes GA
"A Dictionary of Australian Colloquialisms"   1978
Sydney University Press, Sydney

2. Pearsall J, Ed
"The New Oxford Dictionary of English"   1998
Clarendon Press, Oxford

3. Anon
"Australian Slang Dictionary"   2004
Koala net
http://www.koalanet.com.au/australian-slang.html

4. Australian Broadcasting Corporation (ABC)
"Classic FM Breakfast – Word of the Day"   2004
http://www.abc.net.au/classic/breakfast/alpha.htm

5. Schmarr G
"Aussie Slang"   1999
http://members.ozemail.com.au/~enigman/australia/slang.html

6. The University of Queensland Web Page   2004
http://www.uq.edu.au/~mlwham/banjo/biography.html